Student Study Guide

to Accompany

Exceptional Children
An Introduction to Special Education

Eighth Edition

William L. Heward
The Ohio State University

Prepared by

Sheila R. Alber
University of Southern Mississippi

David F. Bicard
Hawthorne Country Day School, Hawthorne, New York

Charles L. Wood
The Ohio State University

PEARSON

Merrill
Prentice Hall

Upper Saddle River, New Jersey
Columbus, Ohio

Pearson Education Ltd.
Pearson Education Singapore Pte. Ltd.
Pearson Education Canada, Ltd.
Pearson Education—Japan

Pearson Education Australia Pty. Limited
Pearson Education North Asia Ltd.
Pearson Educación de Mexico, S.A. de C.V.
Pearson Education Malaysia Pte. Ltd.

10 9 8 7 6 5 4 3
ISBN: 0-13-171215-2

INTRODUCTION

TO THE STUDENT

We have prepared this study guide to the eighth edition of William Heward's textbook *Exceptional Children: An Introduction to Special Education* with you, the student, in mind. This comprehensive review of your textbook's content should provide you with a useful resource for learning about exceptional children, their families, and the field of special education. You will discover that there is a great deal to learn about exceptional children and that mastery of this subject requires diligent study. Our goal is to have this study guide contribute to your success in this very important topic—understanding and teaching exceptional children.

USING THIS STUDY GUIDE

This study guide is divided into chapters corresponding to those in your textbook, and each chapter consists of seven sections: Focus Questions, Essential Concepts, Objectives, Chapter at a Glance, Guided Review, Homework, and Self-Check Quiz. Many chapters include an eighth section: CD-ROM Questions. We have provided suggestions for using the various sections of the Student Study Guide's chapters to assist you in planning and organizing your study routines so that you may attain mastery of your textbook's content.

FOCUS QUESTIONS

Each chapter in your textbook begins with a series of Focus Questions. In the Study Guide, we provide a brief discussion that responds to each question. You will find that the Focus Questions do not necessarily deal with specific details as much as they address larger issues and concepts that have general importance to a category of exceptionality or to the field of special education as a whole. You may find the Focus Questions useful as an introduction to your reading of a chapter or as a review of the chapter's content.

ESSENTIAL CONCEPTS

The Essential Concepts section provides an overview of the key points for each chapter. It may be helpful to read the essential concepts prior to reading the chapter.

OBJECTIVES

Objectives are provided for each chapter to guide your study of the critical information presented in the chapter. You may read the objectives prior to reading the chapter to focus your study on the most important information.

CHAPTER AT A GLANCE

The Chapter at a Glance feature is a quick reference to the main topics, key points, and key terms in each of the textbook's chapters. As with the Focus Questions, you may find the Chapter at a Glance useful as a review or an introduction to each chapter.

GUIDED REVIEW

The Guided Review is designed so that you may complete it while you read the chapter. It allows you to respond actively to the information in the textbook, and it focuses your attention on important points and details from the chapter. Additionally, it provides a useful set of notes to study. You may check the accuracy of your responses to the Guided Review by referring to the companion website.

HOMEWORK

The homework assignments are also included in the Instructor's Manual. Your instructor may require you to complete one of the homework assignments listed for each chapter in your study guide. The homework assignments require you to apply your knowledge by writing a position paper discussing a particular issue related to the chapter's content or to design instruction related to the disability category you are studying.

CD-ROM QUESTIONS

Exceptional Teachers is a multimedia interactive CD-ROM packaged with the *Exceptional Children*, Eighth Edition, textbook. The CD-ROM includes 54 video clips with supporting commentary, artifacts, and discussion questions developed in collaboration with dozens of general education and special education teachers at six schools. The content of the CD-ROM is integrated throughout the text at points identified by a CD-ROM icon in the chapter narrative and in some of the Featured Teacher essays and Teaching & Learning boxes.

As you use the CD-ROM, you will see some of the teachers in the text in action. These teachers (from six different schools) work in a variety of classroom settings to engage students in learning using research-based strategies discussed in the text.

Each of the six schools has nine video clips (a total of 54 videos). Examples of the type of footage you will see include: a kindergarten teacher using choral responding to conduct a classwide morning warm-up activity, collaborative learning activities in an inclusive middle school science classroom, a teacher using puppets to help preschoolers with disabilities learn language and social skills, a parent-teacher conference, and an IEP meeting.

Each of the video clips on the CD-ROM also includes two audio commentaries by the teachers or the authors of the CD-ROM (Bill Heward and Charles Wood). These commentaries help you to synthesize and connect video footage to chapter content and current trends in the field.

Several chapters in the Student Study/Media Guide contain open-ended questions that allow you to reflect upon video clips and audio commentaries and make connections to chapter content.

SELF-CHECK QUIZ

Each chapter also includes a self-check quiz so that you may check your knowledge and comprehension of the content presented in the chapter. An answer key is provided for each of the quizzes at the end of study guide so that you may check the accuracy of your responses.

Contents

CHAPTER ONE
THE PURPOSE AND PROMISE OF SPECIAL EDUCATION

Focus Questions

- ### When is special education needed? How do we know?

Determining the need for special education is a complex and controversial task that is influenced largely by one's views of the purposes of special and general education programs. Basically, special education is needed when the physical attributes and/or learning abilities of students differ from the norm to such an extent that an individual educational program is required to meet their needs. How is the need for special education determined? The need is readily apparent for some students—their academic, physical, and/or social deficits or excesses are obvious. With other students, the need is not so obvious. Highly skilled and dedicated general education teachers working with other specialists and concerned parents are needed to identify students' needs and to provide specialized services.

- ### If categorical labels do not tell us what and how to teach, why are they used in special education?

Some educators argue that a system of classifying children with exceptionalities is a prerequisite to providing the special programs these children require. Labeling allows advocates to make the needs of exceptional children more visible to the public, helps professionals communicate with one another, and may lead to a protective response from peers. Other educators propose alternative approaches to classifying exceptional children that focus on educationally relevant variables, like the curriculum and skill areas that they need to learn.

- ### Why have court cases and federal legislation been required to ensure that children with disabilities receive an appropriate education?

Providing equal educational opportunities and services for children with disabilities closely parallels the struggle by minority groups to gain access to and enjoy the rights to which all Americans are entitled. An awareness of the barriers that have deprived these children of equal educational opportunity is important. Some people believe that special education is too expensive and that many children with exceptionalities cannot benefit from educational programming. Judicial and legislative action has been necessary to establish universal rights for children with disabilities. Our work as special educators is most often performed in local schools, but it is supported and guided by federal and state law.

- ### How can a special educator provide all three kinds of intervention—preventative, remedial, and compensatory—on behalf of an individual child?

Special educators can and do provide all three types of intervention for children with exceptionalities and their families. Preventative efforts are relatively new, and their effects will not likely be felt for many years. In the meantime, we must count on remedial and compensatory efforts to help people with disabilities achieve fuller and more independent lives.

- ### What do you think are the three most important challenges facing special education today? Why? Read your answer again after finishing this book.

This question is best answered by reviewing the current challenges presented in this and other chapters in the text. When responding to this question, consider local, state, and national perspectives—each level of service delivery presents unique challenges. In addition, the attitudes and behavior of people without disabilities toward those with disabilities must be considered in meeting the challenges that face special education today.

Essential Concepts

- Exceptional children differ from normal children to such an extent that an individualized education program is required to meet their educational needs. On one end of the spectrum are children with severe disabilities and on the other are children who demonstrate outstanding academic or artistic achievement. But most important, they are our mothers, fathers, brothers, sisters, cousins, aunts, uncles, and maybe even some of the people in this class.

- The four largest categories of exceptional children are learning disabilities, speech and language impairments, mental retardation, and emotional disturbance. The vast majority of children receiving special education have mild disabilities, and approximately 75% of students with disabilities receive at least part of their education in regular classrooms.

- Special education is an outgrowth of the civil rights movement of the late 1960s and early 1970s. In a piece of landmark legislation, PL 94-142, the federal government established that a free and appropriate education is the right of all students. Special education continues to evolve with each passage of related federal legislation; among the most recent laws to have a potentially huge impact is the No Child Left Behind Act.

- Special education consists of purposeful intervention efforts at three different levels: preventive, remedial, and compensatory. It is individually planned, specialized, intensive, goal-directed instruction. When practiced most effectively and ethically, special education is also characterized by the use of research-based teaching methods and guided by direct and frequent measures of student performance.

- As a potential future educator, do not become overwhelmed by the current challenges facing the field. Special educators do not face these challenges alone; general education, other social and adult service agencies, and society as a whole must help meet these challenges.

Objectives

WHO ARE EXCEPTIONAL CHILDREN?
1. List the defining characteristics of exceptional children.
2. Define and describe *impairment*, *disability*, and *handicap*.
3. Define and describe children who are at risk for developing disabilities.

HOW MANY EXCEPTIONAL CHILDREN ARE THERE?
1. List the reasons why it is difficult to determine the precise number of exceptional children.
2. List the percentage of school age children receiving special education services.
3. List the percentage of exceptional children representing the four largest categories.

WHY DO WE LABEL AND CLASSIFY EXCEPTIONAL CHILDREN?
1. List the benefits of labeling.
2. List the disadvantages of labeling.
3. List the alternatives to labeling.

WHY ARE LAWS GOVERNING THE EDUCATION OF EXCEPTIONAL CHILDREN NECESSARY?
1. Describe how exceptional children have been excluded in the past.
2. Describe why the *Brown v. Board of Education of Topeka* set precedent for special education.
3. Describe the *PARC* case and identify its importance in determining equal protection for exceptional children.

THE INDIVIDUALS WITH DISABILITEIS EDUCATION ACT
1. Define and describe the six major principles of IDEA.
2. Describe how special education is funded.
3. Describe how Section 504 of the Rehabilitation Act of 1973 has affected special education.
4. List the four key principles of the No Child Left Behind Act.

WHAT IS SPECIAL EDUCATION?
1. Compare (describe the similarities) and contrast (describe the differences) the different perspectives of special education.
2. List the features of and describe special education as intervention.
3. List the features of and describe special education as instruction.
4. List the defining features of special education.

CURRENT AND FUTURE CHALLENGES
1. Define and describe the four critical areas in the field of special education.

Chapter One at a Glance

Main Topics	Key Points	Key Terms
The Purpose and Promise of Special Education	Exceptional children are those whose physical attributes and/or learning abilities differ from the norm (either below or above) to such an extent that they require an individualized program of special education.	exceptional children impairment disability handicap at-risk
Who Are Exceptional Children?	An impairment refers to the loss or reduced function of a body part or organ.	
	A disability exists when an impairment limits the ability to perform certain tasks.	
	Handicap refers to problems encountered when interacting with the environment.	
	At-risk refers to children who have a greater-than-usual chance of developing a disability.	
How Many Exceptional Children Are There?	It is impossible to state the precise number of children with disabilities because of different criteria across states used for identification and for the assessment of the effectiveness of preventative services, and the imprecise nature of assessment.	
	Children in special education represent about 9% of the school-age population.	
	The four largest categories are learning disabilities, speech and language impairments, mental retardation, and emotional disturbance.	
	Approximately 75% of students with disabilities receive at least part of their education in regular classrooms.	
Why Do We Label and Classify Exceptional Children?	Some believe that disability labels can have a negative effect on the child and others' perception of her and can lead to exclusion; while others believe that labeling is a necessary first step to providing needed intervention and that labels are important for comparing and communicating about research findings.	curriculum-based assessment
	Children can be classified according to the curriculum and skill areas they need to learn. In curriculum-based assessment, students are assessed and classified relative to the degree to which they are learning specific curriculum content.	
Why Are Laws Governing the Education of Exceptional Children Necessary?	Children who are different have had a history of being denied full and fair access to educational opportunities.	
	Special education was strongly influenced by social developments and court decisions in the 1950s and 1960s.	

Chapter One at a Glance

Main Topics	Key Points	Key Terms
The Individuals with Disabilities Education Act	The Individuals with Disabilities Education Act encompasses six major principles: zero reject; nondiscriminatory identification and evaluation; a right to a free, appropriate education; education in the least restrictive environment; due process safeguards; and parent and student participation and shared decision making.	zero reject least restrictive environment IEP due process IFSP related services assistive technology
	Special education law has also extended special education services to infants, toddlers, and preschoolers.	
	The Gifted and Talented Children's Education Act of 1978 provides financial incentives for state and local education agencies to develop programs for students who are gifted.	
	Section 504 of the Rehabilitation Act of 1973 forbids discrimination in all federally funded programs, including educational and vocational programs, on the basis of disability.	
	The Americans with Disabilities Act extends civil rights protection of persons with disabilities to private sector employment, all public services, public accommodations, transportation, and telecommunications.	
What Is Special Education?	Special education consists of purposeful intervention efforts at three different levels: preventative, remedial, and compensatory.	preventative primary prevention secondary prevention tertiary prevention remedial rehabilitation compensatory
	Special education is individually planned, specialized, intensive, goal-directed instruction.	
	When practiced most effectively and ethically, special education is also characterized by the use of research-based teaching methods and guided by direct and frequent measures of student performance.	
Current and Future Challenges	There exists a gap between what research has discovered about teaching and learning and what is practiced in many classrooms.	
	The recent growth in providing special education and family-focused services for infants, toddlers, and preschoolers who have disabilities or are at risk for developmental delay is a positive sign. Increased efforts must be made to make these services more widely available.	
	Other current and future challenges are to improve students' transition from school to adult life, and to improve the special education–general education partnership.	

Guided Review

I. Who Are Exceptional Children?

- Exceptional children differ from the norm (either below or above) to such an extent that they

  require _____

  _____

- The term *exceptional children* refers _____

  _____

  _____

- *Impairment* refers to the _____

- Disability exists when an impairment limits the ability to _____

  _____

- *Handicap* refers to a problem or disadvantage that a person with a disability encounters

  _____

- *At risk* refers to children who _____

II. How Many Exceptional Children Are There?

- More than 6.3 million children and youth with disabilities, ages 3 to 21, received special education during the 2003–2004 school year.

III. Why Do We Label and Classify Exceptional Children?

A. Possible Benefits of Labeling

- Recognizes _____

- May lead to a _____

- Helps professionals _____

- Funding and resources are based on _____

- Labels help advocacy groups _____

- Makes special needs more _____

B. Possible Disadvantages of Labeling

- Focuses on _____

6

- May stigmatize the student and lead to _____

- May negatively affect _____

- May cause others to hold lower _____

- Performance deficits often acquire the role of _____

- Diminishes each child's _____

- Built-in excuse for _____

- Disproportionate number of _____

- Special education labels have a certain _____

- Requires great expenditure that might be better spent on _____

C. Alternatives to Labeling

- Curriculum-based assessment: _____
  _____

IV. Why Are Laws Governing the Education of Exceptional Children Necessary?

A. An Exclusionary Past

- Children who are different have often been denied_____
  _____

B. Separate Is Not Equal

- Special education was strongly influenced by social developments and court decisions in the 1950s and 1960s (e.g., *Brown v. Board of Education*)

C. Equal Protection

- All children are entitled to a free, appropriate education

V. The Individuals with Disabilities Education Act

A. Six Major Principles of IDEA

- Zero Reject:_____

- Nondiscriminatory Identification and Evaluation: _____
  _____
  _____

- Free, Appropriate Education: _____

- Least Restrictive Environment: _____

  _____

- Due Process Safeguards: _____

- Parent and Student Participation and Shared Decision Making: _____

  _____

B. Other Provisions of IDEA

- Extending Special Education Services to Infants, Toddlers, and Preschoolers: Individual Family Service Plans

- Related Services and Assistive Technology

- Federal Funding of Special Education

C. Legal Challenges Based on IDEA

- Extended School Year: _____

- Related Services: _____

- Disciplining Students with Disabilities: _____

  _____

- Right to Education: _____

D. Related Legislation

- The Gifted and Talented Children's Education Act of 1978 provides _____

  _____

- The Jacob K Javits Gifted and Talented Student Education Act (1988) specified funds be

  directed towards _____

  _____

- Section 504 of the Rehabilitation Act of 1973 extends civil rights to_____

  _____

- The Americans with Disabilities Act (1990) extends civil rights to _____

  _____

E. No Child Left Behind Act

- Accountability: _____

- Flexibility and local control: _____

  _____

- Enhanced parental choice: _____

  _____

- Focuses on what works: _____

  _____

- Implications for students with disabilities

VI. What Is Special Education?

- Preventative Intervention: _____

- Remedial Intervention: _____

- Compensatory Intervention: _____

A. Special Education as Instruction

- Who: _____

  _____

- What: _____

- How: _____

- _____

- Where: _____

  _____

B. Defining Features of Special Education

- Special education is _____

VII. Current and Future Challenges

A. Close the Research-to-Practice Gap

B. Increase the availability and intensity of early intervention and prevention programs

C. Improve students' transition from school to adult life

D. Improve the Special Education–General Education Partnership

Homework _____

Write a 2- to 3-page paper on one of the following topics.

1. Read the Prologue and Postscript and discuss your own philosophy of education.

2. "What's in a Name? The Labels and Language of Special Education," in the Profiles & Perspectives module on the Companion Website, presents an enlightening commentary on the challenge and importance of changing attitudes and values toward individuals with disabilities. Write a paper addressing the following questions: How does the practice of changing labels affect people with and without disabilities? How can the use of labels both help and hinder children with exceptionalities?

3. Think about the teachers you had when you were in elementary school and high school. The teachers that immediately come to mind might be your exceptionally good teachers or exceptionally bad teachers. Write a list of characteristics of your good teachers. Examine your list and prioritize in sequential order the most important attributes of effective teachers. Write an explanation for why you believe each characteristic you selected is important.

Self-Check Quiz _____

True/False

1. About as many males as females receive special education services.

2. Most agree that special education labeling should be rejected because of its disadvantages.

3. IDEA applies to gifted and talented children.

4. The term *at risk* refers to children with a greater-than-usual chance of developing a disability.

5. Just as there is regular and special education, there are two distinct kinds of children: the "regular" and the "exceptional."

6. All children with disabilities, without exception, have the right to a free, appropriate program of public education in the least restrictive environment.

7. Public Law 94-142, the Education for all Handicapped Children Act, and the Individuals with Disabilities Education Act are all the same law, as reauthorized and amended by Congress over the years.

8. A person with an impairment has a disability, as those terms are used in special education.

9. The term *exceptional children* refers to those whose physical and/or learning abilities are below the norm to such an extent that special education is necessary for the child to benefit fully from education.

10. A student becomes eligible for special education because of identified membership in a given category.

11. Federal funding reimburses states for the majority of expenses related to provision of special education services.

12. As related services, children with disabilities are entitled to things such as special transportation and counseling if needed to access and benefit from special education.

13. P.L. 99-457 mandated early intervention services to infants and toddlers with disabilities and their families.

14. If a private school placement is needed in order to appropriately educate a student, the placement is made at school expense.

15. Most students are receiving special education services under the category of learning disabilities.

Essay Questions

1. Compare and contrast the terms *impairment*, *disability*, and *handicap*.

2. Describe due process safeguards.

CHAPTER TWO
PLANNING AND PROVIDING SPECIAL EDUCATION SERVICES

Focus Questions _____

- **Why must the planning and provision of special education be so carefully sequenced and evaluated?**

  The general goal for special education services is to increase the likelihood that students with disabilities function as independently as possible in normalized settings. Children with disabilities tend to function below grade level and usually take longer to master essential skills. Therefore, it is important that teachers deliver instruction both effectively and efficiently. Target skills must be carefully selected and sequenced so students attain mastery. Additionally, skills must be evaluated and monitored daily so that teachers can make timely instructional decisions. If the student is progressing at an appropriate rate, the teacher can assume that the instructional intervention is effective and should continue using the intervention. If the student is not progressing as expected, the teacher can quickly modify instruction to attain the desired outcomes.

- **Why does the effectiveness of special education depend on collaboration and teaming?**

  An appropriate education for students with disabilities can best be accomplished when both regular and special education teachers and other service providers work together to provide high-quality instruction for all children. The educational needs of exceptional children cannot be resolved by any single individual or professional discipline. Children with disabilities deserve the collective and collaborative efforts of all individuals charged with the responsibility of educating them.

- **How should the quality of a student's individualized education program be judged?**

  The individualized education program (IEP) is the centerpiece of the special education process. IDEA requires that an IEP be developed and implemented for every student with disabilities between the ages of 3 and 21. The IEP is a system for spelling out where the child is, where he should be going, how he will get there, how long it will take, and how to tell when he has arrived. The IEP is a measure of accountability for teachers and schools. Whether or not a particular school or educational program is effective will be judged, to some extent, by how well it is able to help children meet the goals and objectives set forth in their IEPs.

- **Is the least restrictive environment always the regular classroom? Why?**

  The regular classroom is often, but not always, the least restrictive environment. The general education classroom is the starting point for the IEP team's discussion of placement. Judgments about the restrictiveness of a given setting must always be made in relation to the individual needs of the student as well as the needs of other students. The regular classroom can promote or restrict a child's educational opportunities and skill development depending on the quality of the learning opportunities the child receives. No setting is, in and of itself, restrictive or nonrestrictive. It is the needs of the child and the degree to which a particular setting meets those needs which defines restrictiveness. Restrictiveness is a feature of place. But the physical place in which children receive their education will rarely be the only variable that determines the appropriateness of their educational opportunities.

- **What elements must be in place for special education to be appropriate in inclusive classrooms?**

Studies have shown that well-planned, carefully conducted inclusion can be generally effective with students of all ages, types, and degrees of disability. In order for an inclusive placement to be successful, collaboration and teaming are crucial. Professionals who are well-trained in inclusive practices can work together to solve learning and behavior problems. Inclusive education would probably be appropriate for many children under these circumstances.

Essential Concepts

- This chapter focuses on four general topics: the individualized education program (IEP), the concept of least restrictive environment, teaming and collaboration, and special education reform.

- PL 94-142 requires that every child receiving special education services has a detailed written plan to guide those services and their delivery. This plan, called an individualized education program (IEP), is cooperatively developed by the school and the child's parents. Although an IEP is not legally binding, it is intended to establish a high degree of accountability for meeting the child's needs.

- At the head of PL 94-142 is the concept of appropriateness and the presumption that what constitutes an appropriate education for one student is not necessarily appropriate for another. The issue of appropriateness cannot be decided solely on the basis of where a student receives his or her education. The restrictiveness of a particular setting should be assessed in relation to the needs of the child. An educational environment must support the academic and social behavior of the teacher, the regular education students, and students with disabilities. The teacher's obligation to teach and all students' opportunities to learn should not be dominated or controlled by any one individual or group.

- Both regular and special educators are responsible for insuring that the needs of exceptional children are met. Effective educational programs must be cooperatively and collaboratively planned and implemented. Individuals considering a career in education can expect to be involved in teaching exceptional children to some degree.

- The passage of PL 94-142 brought to an end the wholesale and often arbitrary exclusion of children with disabilities from the full range of experiences available in the public schools. These reforms encourage the school to fit the student rather than have the student fit the school, and they are likely to go a long way toward improving the education of all children. The challenge remains, however, about how to best meet the needs of exceptional children. While there is little disagreement that education is part of the answer, answers to questions about the content and organization of that education will determine the direction and future of special education.

Objectives

THE PROCESS OF SPECIAL EDUCATION
1. Define and describe the process of prereferral intervention.
2. Define and describe MFE.
3. Define and describe the process of NDE.
4. List the factors that may contribute to culturally and linguistically diverse children being both under- and overrepresented in special education.

COLLABORATION AND TEAMING
1. Define and provide examples of the different teaming models.

INDIVIDUALIZED EDUCATION PROGRAM
1. List the members of the IEP team.
2. List the components of an IEP.

LEAST RESTRICTIVE ENVIRONMENT
1. Define LRE.
2. Describe the process of determining the LRE.

INCLUSIVE EDUCATION
1. Discuss the arguments for and against full inclusion.

WHERE DOES SPECIAL EDUCATION GO FROM HERE?
1. Discuss the challenges that special education faces in the future.

Chapter Two at a Glance

Main Topics	Key Points	Key Terms
Planning and Providing Special Education Services	IDEA mandates a particular sequence of events that schools must follow in identifying and educating children with disabilities.	prereferral intervention intervention assistance teams evaluation team multidisciplinary team child study team
The Process of Special Education	Prereferral intervention is an informal, problem-solving process with two primary purposes: to provide immediate instructional and/or behavioral assistance, and to reduce the chances of identifying a child for special education who may not be disabled.	
	Many schools use intervention assistance teams to help classroom teachers devise and implement adaptations.	
	IDEA requires that all children suspected of having a disability receive a nondiscriminatory, multifactored evaluation.	
	If a child is eligible to receive special education services, an individualized educational program must be developed. The IEP team must also determine the least restrictive environment for the student.	
Collaboration and Teaming	Coordination, consultation, and teaming are three modes of collaboration that team members can use.	coordination consultation teaming interdisciplinary teams transdisciplinary teams
	Multidisciplinary teams are composed of professionals from different disciplines who work independently of one another.	
	Interdisciplinary teams are characterized by formal channels of communication between members.	
	Transdisciplinary teams seek to provide services in a uniform and integrated fashion.	
Individualized Education Program	IDEA requires that an IEP be developed and implemented for every student with disabilities between the ages of 3 and 21.	individualized education program IEP team individualized family services plan (IFSP) individualized transition plan
	Individualized family service plans are developed for infants and toddlers from birth to age 3.	
	The IEP team must include the following members: parents, regular education teacher, special education teacher, LEA representative, an individual who can interpret evaluation results, others at the discretion of the parent or school, and the student (age 14 or older must be invited).	
	IEP components include present levels of educational performance, annual goals and short-term objectives, special education and related services, supplementary aids and services, and projected beginning and ending dates. Transition goals must be included when the child reaches age 14.	

Chapter Two at a Glance

Main Topics	Key Points	Key Terms
Least Restrictive Environment	Least restrictive environment means that, to the maximum extent appropriate, children with disabilities should be educated with children without disabilities.	least restrictive environment continuum of services resource room residential facility
	LRE is the setting that is closest to a regular school program and that also meets the child's special education needs.	
	The continuum of services is a range of placement and service options to meet the individual needs of students with disabilities.	
	Before considering if instruction and related services will be delivered in any setting other than the regular classroom, the IEP team must discuss if the annual goals and short-term objectives can be achieved in the regular classroom.	
	Removal of a child from the regular classroom should take place only when the nature and severity of the disability is such that an appropriate education in that setting cannot be achieved.	
Inclusive Education	Inclusion means educating students with disabilities in regular classrooms.	inclusion
	Studies have shown that well-planned, carefully conducted inclusion can be generally effective with students of all ages, types, and degrees of disability.	
	A few special educators believe that the LRE principle should give way to full inclusion, in which all students with disabilities are placed full-time in regular classrooms.	
	Most special educators and professional organizations, such as CEC, support inclusion as a goal but believe that the continuum of services and program options must be maintained and that placement decisions must be based on the student's individual education needs.	
Where Does Special Education Go from Here?	The promise of a free, appropriate public education for all children with disabilities is an ambitious one, but substantial progress has been made toward fulfillment of that promise.	
	Implementation of IDEA has brought problems of funding, inadequate teacher training, and opposition by some to inclusion of children with disabilities in regular classrooms.	
	Regardless of where services are delivered, the most crucial variable is the quality of instruction that each child receives.	

Guided Review

I. The Process of Special Education

    A. Prereferral Intervention

        • Prereferral intervention is an informal, problem-solving process with two primary purposes:

        _____

        _____

        • Many schools use intervention assistance teams to help classroom teachers devise and

        _____

    B. Evaluation and Identification

        • IDEA requires that all children suspected of having a disability receive a _____

        _____

        • Technically sound instruments must be used to assess students across four domains: _____

        _____

        • Tests must not discriminate on the basis of_____

        • Tests must be administered in the child's _____

        • Standardized tests must have been _____

        • Standardized tests must be administered by _____

        • The child is assessed in _____

        • The evaluation process must not rely on _____

    C. Program Planning

        • If a child is eligible to receive special education services, _____

        _____

        • The IEP process determines _____

        _____

        _____

    D. Placement

        • The IEP team must also determine the _____

E. Review and Evaluation

- The IEP must be thoroughly and formally reviewed on a(n) _____ basis.

- The IEP document has limited usefulness without _____

_____

II. Collaboration and Teaming

- Coordination: _____

_____

- Consultation: _____

A. Teaming

- Multidisciplinary teams are_____

_____

- Interdisciplinary teams are _____

- Transdisciplinary teams seek _____

B. Co-Teaching

- One teaching/one helping

- Parallel teaching

- Station teaching

- Alternative teaching

- Team teaching

III. Individualized Education Program

- IDEA requires that an IEP be developed and implemented for every student with disabilities

  between the ages of _____

- Individualized family service plans are developed for_____

A. IEP Team

- The IEP team must include the following members: _____

_____

B. IEP Components

- A statement of _____ of educational performance

- A statement of _____ and short-term objectives

- A statement of special education and related services, and _____

- An explanation of the extent to which the student will not _____

  _____

- Individual modifications

- The projected date for the _____

- A statement of how the child will be assessed

IEPs for older students must also include _____

C. IEP Functions and Formats

- IEP formats vary widely across school districts, and schools may _____

  _____

D. Problems and Potential Solutions

- Properly including all of the mandated components in an IEP is no guarantee that the

  _____

- Special and regular educators are working together to create procedures for developing IEPs

  that go beyond compliance with the law and _____

  _____

IV. Least Restrictive Environment

- Least restrictive environment means that to the maximum extent appropriate, _____

  _____

- LRE is the setting that is closest to a regular school program and also _____

  _____

A. A Continuum of Services

- The continuum of services is _____

  _____

B. Determining the LRE

- Before considering that instruction and related services will be delivered in any setting other than the regular classroom, the IEP team must discuss _____ _____

- Removal of a child from the regular classroom should take place only when _____ _____ _____

- Placement must not be regarded as _____

V. Inclusive Education

- Inclusion means educating students with disabilities in _____

- Cooperative learning activities provide a strategic approach for integrating students with disabilities into _____

A. Four Evidence-Based Models

- Peer assisted learning strategies (PALS)

- Juniper Gardens Children's project (CWPT)

- SUNY Fredonia Classwide Student Tutoring Teams (CSTT)

- The Ohio State University CWPT Model

B. Characteristics Common to All Four Models

- Clearly defined _____

- Individual _____

- High rates of _____

- Immediate _____

- Systematic error correction

- Measurement of _____

- Motivation for students

C. Arguments For and Against Full Inclusion

- Legitimates _____

- Confuses segregation and integration with _____

- Is based on a _____

- Supports the primacy of _____

- Sanctions infringements of people's rights

- Implies that people must move as they _____

- Directs attention to physical settings rather than _____

- Most special educators are *not* in favor of _____

  _____

VI. Where Does Special Education Go from Here?

- The promise of a free, appropriate public education for all children with disabilities is an

  ambitious one, but substantial progress has been made towards _____

- Implementation of IDEA has brought problems of _____

  _____

- Regardless of where services are delivered, the most crucial variable is the _____

  _____

Homework

Write a 2- to 3-page paper on one of the following topics.

1. List and prioritize the information necessary to determine the least restrictive environment for a child with disabilities. Then write a hypothetical case study describing the social, academic, and behavioral characteristics of the child. Include information on the child's age, grade, ethnicity, and specific strengths and weaknesses. Additionally, describe the characteristics of the child's school environment (e.g., teacher training in inclusive education, types of supports in place, demographic information on nondisabled peers). Based on the information you provided, select the least restrictive environment for this child, and defend the appropriateness of your decision.

2. Discuss the extent to which students with disabilities should be educated in regular classrooms. Should students with disabilities be fully included in regular classrooms for the entire school day or should a student's placement be individually determined using the continuum of placement options? Explain the reasons for your opinion. Issues that may be addressed in this paper include: the advantages and disadvantages of inclusion for students with and without disabilities, labeling issues, separation and stigma issues, and social and educational outcomes of students with disabilities.

CD-ROM Questions

1. Describe how collaboration between a special education teacher and a general education teacher can improve school success for students with disabilities.

   School: Dunkirk Middle School
   Videos and Commentaries: Mary & Jean, Team Meeting, & University Partnership

2. What are the critical elements that make cooperative learning strategies such as Think Pair Share and Numbered Heads Together effective?

   School: Dunkirk Middle School
   Videos and Commentaries: Heads Together, Pair Share, & University Partnership

3. What makes inclusion effective for students with disabilities?

   School: Dunkirk Middle School
   Videos and Commentaries: Heads Together, Pair Share, Response Cards, Response System, & University Partnership

4. How and when does inclusion become "more than a place"?

   School: Oakstone Academy
   Videos and Commentaries: All

5. What are the characteristics of a good IEP team?

   School: Dunkirk Elementary School
   Videos and Commentaries: IEP Meeting

6. Describe a peer tutoring procedure students could use to teach science vocabulary and concepts to one another.

   Schools: Como Elementary School & Oakstone Academy
   Videos and Commentaries: Tutoring Procedures, Tutoring Group, Test Group, & Peer Tutoring

Self-Check Quiz

True/False

1. Required members of an IEP team include the child's parents and the child, if age 14 or older.

2. IEP formats are dictated by law, and schools may not go beyond those requirements in the information they include.

3. IEPs must state how the child's progress toward annual goals will be measured.

4. Prereferral intervention is a required component of IDEA.

5. One argument against inclusion is that even the most knowledgeable and dedicated teachers in regular classrooms have students who fail to respond to the best practices implemented.

6. A multidisciplinary team is composed of professionals from different disciplines who work independently of one another.

7. According to Giangreco and other full-inclusion advocates, inclusion is about restructuring education for all students, rather than specifically being about those with disabilities.

8. Teachers commonly refer children for minor learning problems, the majority not qualifying when evaluated for special education.

9. Terrill has an illness that prevents him from attending school; IDEA allows him to receive services at home or in a hospital.

10. *Least restrictive environment* and *inclusion* are synonymous terms.

11. Beginning at age 14, a child's IEP must address transition needs.

12. A child's parents are a part of a school-based evaluation team.

13. IDEA states that goals and objectives on an IEP must be developed by the special education teacher.

14. The intent of LRE is to best fit students into programs.

15. Individualized education programs must be formally, thoroughly reviewed every year.

Essay Questions

1. Discuss the importance of collaboration.

2. Discuss the ways in which a student can participate in assessment, the IEP conference, and instruction.

CHAPTER THREE
COLLABORATING WITH PARENTS AND FAMILIES IN A CULTURALLY AND LINGUISTICALLY DIVERSE SOCIETY

*Focus Questions*_____

- **What can a teacher learn from the family of a child with disabilities?**

For the vast majority of children, parents are their first teachers. In addition, parents know their children best. It therefore would be short-sighted for educators not to develop productive parent-teacher partnerships. What teachers can learn from the parents and families of children with disabilities is as varied as the children themselves. Some parents will have a great deal to offer by providing a deeper understanding of the overall needs of their child, helping identify meaningful instructional objectives, encouraging extra practice of skills at home, and teaching their children new skills themselves. Other parents may be less involved in their child's education but can still provide important insight about the educational needs of their children.

- **In what ways can a child's disability affect the family system and roles of parents?**

The birth of any child causes changes in a family. However, families of children with a disability may experience added stress. Evidence suggests that many families of children with disabilities go through an adjustment process, trying to work through their feelings. Educators should refrain from expecting parents or family members to exhibit any kind of "typical" reaction. However, almost all parents and family members can be helped by sensitive and supportive friends and professionals.

- **How can a teacher who is not the parent of a child with a disability communicate effectively and meaningfully with parents of exceptional children?**

Educators who are not parents of a child with disabilities cannot know the 24-hour reality of being the parent of a child with disabilities or chronic illness. Nonetheless, they should strive for an awareness and understanding of how a child with special needs affects (and is affected by) the family system. This increased awareness of the challenges a family of a child with disabilities faces is the first step to effective and meaningful parent-teacher communication.

- **How can a teacher communicate effectively and meaningfully with families from diverse cultures?**

Although some would suggest that good teachers are born, not made, there are many skills required of classroom professionals that are acquired through experience over time. Culturally responsive assessment, curriculum, and instructional procedures will not become realities until teachers learn to appreciate diversity. The first step in becoming culturally responsive is to develop a general self-awareness and appreciation of diversity. This process begins with a thorough understanding and appreciation of one's own culture but must then be extended to an understanding, appreciation, and respect of the culture of others.

- **How much parent and family involvement is enough?**

In general, the more involved the parents are in their child's education, the better. Sometimes, however, the time and energy required for parents to participate in home-based tutoring programs or parent education groups cause stress among family members or guilt if parents cannot fulfill teachers' expectations. The Mirror Model for Parental Involvement recognizes that parents have a great deal to offer, as well as a need to receive services from special educators. All parents should be expected to provide and obtain information, most parents will be active participants in IEP planning, and fewer parents will participate or contribute to workshops and extended parent education groups.

Essential Concepts

- Parents and family members are the best advocates and the first teachers. Parents are indispensable partners in the educational process. They want to be involved in their child's education. The family is likely to be the only group of adults involved with a child's educational program throughout his or her entire school career. In addition, research and practice has shown that educational programs are more effective when parents are involved.

- It is important for teachers to recognize that there are many, sometimes difficult roles that parents must fulfill. These roles include caregiver, financial provider, teacher, counselor, parent of siblings without a disability, marriage partner, and advocate.

- Effective parent-teacher partnerships are characterized by family members and professionals jointly pursuing shared goals in a climate of mutual respect. Regular two-way communication with parents is the key operational element of an effective parent-teacher partnership.

- Preparation is the key to effective parent-teacher conferences. Preparation for the conference entails establishing specific objectives, obtaining and reviewing the student's grades, selecting examples of the student's work, and preparing for an agenda of the meeting.

- Acknowledging, understanding, and respecting cultural diversity is an essential attribute of every teacher. It is equally important to understand the potential impact of being educated in a system that serves a predominantly Caucasian, middle-class culture on children from culturally diverse backgrounds. With these points in mind, two issues are particularly pertinent in this chapter: (1) every teacher must be responsive to the individual needs of every student; and (2) the fundamental principles of learning and effective instruction are applicable to all children. In other words, good teaching practices will benefit all students, whatever their cultural background.

Objectives

SUPPORT FOR FAMILY INVOLVEMENT
1. List the reasons why family collaboration is a necessary component of special education.
2. Discuss the four factors responsible for increased emphasis on parent and family involvement.
3. Describe the benefits of family involvement for teachers, parents, and the student.

UNDERSTANDING FAMILIES OF CHILDREN WITH DISABILITIES
1. Describe the impact on the family of an exceptional child.
2. Describe the nine roles and responsibility that parents of exceptional children play.
3. Discus the importance of respite care for families of children with severe disabilities.

DEVELOPING AND MAINTAINING FAMILY-PROFESSIONAL PARTNERSHIPS
1. Describe the five principles for effective communication between special education and families.
2. Describe the barriers to parent/teacher collaboration.

WORKING WITH CULTURALLY AND LINGUISTICALLY DIVERSE FAMILIES
1. List and describe the barriers that might exist in working with parents and families from culturally diverse backgrounds.
2. List and describe the factors that may prevent some culturally and linguistically diverse caregivers from becoming actively involved in school partnerships.
3. List the ways in which educators can increase active parent involvement.

METHODS OF HOME-SCHOOL COMMUNICATION
1. List and describe the three most common modes of home-school communication.
2. Discuss the guidelines for working with parents and families of exceptional children.

OTHER FORMS OF PARENT INVOLVEMENT
1. Describe the importance of parent education and support.
2. Describe the guidelines for home-based parent tutoring.
3. Discuss the mirror model of parent involvement.

CURRENT ISSUES AND FUTURE TRENDS
1. Discuss the philosophical foundation for family-centered services.
2. Describe the strength-based approach to family support.

Chapter Three at a Glance

Main Topics	Key Points	Key Terms
Collaborating with Parents and Families in a Diverse Society	Families have the greatest vested interest in their children and are usually the most knowledgeable about their needs. The family is likely to be the only group of adults involved with a child's educational program throughout his or her entire school career.	collaboration
	To meet the special needs of children with disabilities, educators must expand the traditional role of the classroom teacher	
Support for Family Involvement	IDEA requires collaboration between schools and families.	
Understanding Families of Children with Disabilities	Parents go through a period of adjustment when they find out their child has a disability. Educators should refrain from expecting parents to exhibit any kind of "typical" reaction.	respite care advocate
	The roles of the exceptional parent include: caregiver, provider, teacher, counselor, behavior support specialist, parent of siblings without disabilities, marriage partner, information specialist/trainer for significant others, and advocate.	
	Respite care is the short-term care of a family member with disabilities to provide relief for parents from caretaking duties.	
	Parents and families of children with disabilities face new challenges at each stage of their child's development.	
Developing and Maintaining Family-Professional Partnerships	Effective parent-teacher partnerships are characterized by family members and professionals jointly pursuing shared goals in a climate of mutual respect. Regular two-way communication with parents is the key operational element of an effective parent-teacher partnership.	positive behavioral support cultural reciprocity dialoguing
	The following are principles of effective communication: accept parents' statements, listen actively, encourage, and stay focused.	
	Differences in the cultural and linguistic beliefs and practices of professionals and families often serve as barriers to parent involvement.	
	Roadblocks to communication include: treating parents as vulnerable clients, keeping professional distance, treating parents as if they need counseling, blaming parents for their child's condition, disrespecting parents as less intelligent, treating parents as adversaries, and labeling parents.	
	Dialoguing is an approach to conflict resolution in which both parties try to see each other's point of view.	

Chapter Three at a Glance

Main Topics	Key Points	Key Terms
Working with Culturally and Linguistically Diverse Families	Practitioners must understand that parents are "life educated" and know their children better than anyone else. Barriers that might exist in working with parents and families from diverse backgrounds include: language skills, home-school partnerships, work interference, knowledge of the school system, self-confidence, and past experiences. To overcome these barriers, teachers should have a general understanding of the culture, child-rearing practices, family patterns, views of exceptionality, availability and use of community resources, linguistic difference, acknowledging own biases, beliefs about professionals, nonverbal communication styles, view of medical practices, sex roles, and religion.	
Methods of Home-School Communication	Parent-teacher conferences should be scheduled regularly. In a parent-teacher conference, parents and teachers can exchange information and coordinate their efforts to assist the child with disabilities in school and at home. Preparation is the key to effective parent-teacher conferences. A suggested 4-step sequence for parent-teacher conferences is: build rapport, obtain information, provide information, and summarize and follow up. Frequent written messages can be an excellent way of maintaining home-school communication, and short, positive telephone calls from the teacher reduce parents' fear that calls from school always indicate a problem.	happy grams two-way home-school note systems home-school contracts
Other Forms of Parent Involvement	Parents can serve as effective teachers for their children. Guidelines for home-based parent tutoring include the following: keep sessions short, make the experience positive, keep responses to the child consistent, use tutoring to practice and extend skills already learned in school, and keep a record. Parents can also be involved in parent education and support groups, parent to parent groups, and as research partners. The Mirror Model attempts to give parents an equal part in deciding what services they need and what services they might provide.	Mirror Model
Current Issues and Future Trends	Professionals who work with parents should value family needs and support families. Family-centered services are predicated on the belief that the child is part of the family system and that effective change for the child cannot be achieved without helping the entire family.	family-centered services strength-based approach

Guided Review

I. Support for Family Involvement

- Parents want to _____

- Research and practice have shown that educational effectiveness _____

  _____

- The law requires _____

A. Parents: Advocating for Needed Change

  - Families have the greatest vested interest in their children and _____

    _____

B. Educators: Striving for Greater Effectiveness

  - To meet the special needs of children with disabilities, educators must _____

    _____

C. Legislators: Mandating Parent and Family Involvement

  - Each reauthorization of IDEA has _____ parent and
    family participation in the education of children with disabilities.

II. Understanding Families of Children with Disabilities

A. The Impact of a Child with Disabilities on the Family

  - The grief cycle consists of three stages: _____

    _____

  - Educators should refrain from _____

    _____

B. The Many Roles of the Exceptional Parent

  - Caregiver

  - Provider

  - Teacher

  - Counselor

  - Behavior support specialist

- Parent of siblings without disabilities

- Marriage partner

- Information specialist/trainer for significant others

- Advocate

C. Changing Needs as Children Grow

- Parents and families of children with disabilities face new challenges at each stage of their child's development.

III. Developing and Maintaining Family-Professional Partnerships

A. Principles of Effective Communication

- Accepting _____

- Listening _____

- Question _____

- Encourage

- Stay _____

B. Identifying and Breaking Down Barriers to Parent-Teacher Partnerships

- Educators must be responsive to the practices and beliefs of families from diverse cultural backgrounds, and identify and eliminate attitudes and behaviors that block family involvement.

1. Professional Roadblocks to Communication

- Treating parents as _____

- Keeping _____

- Treating parents as if they _____

- Blaming parents for _____

- Disrespecting parents as_____

- Treating parents as _____

- Labeling parents_____

2. Conflict Resolution through Dialoguing

- Dialoguing is an approach to conflict resolution in which both parties _____

  _____

IV. Working with Culturally and Linguistically Diverse Families

    A. Understanding and Respecting Cultural Differences

- Barriers that might exist in working with culturally diverse families: _____

_____

- Many families may be English-language learners, be less well educated, have low socioeconomic status, or be undocumented immigrants.

- Practitioners must understand that parents _____

- If families are suspected to be undocumented immigrants, they are naturally _____

_____

- Families from culturally diverse backgrounds tend to be _____

- Culturally diverse families may have different _____

- The educational system may be extremely _____ to the family

    B. Providing Culturally Responsive Services to Families

- Conduct family interviews

- Cultural reciprocity

V. Methods of Home-School Communication

    A. Parent-Teacher Conferences

- Parent-teacher conferences should be scheduled _____

- Preparation for the conference entails _____

_____

- Conducting the 4-step conference: _____

_____

    B. Written Messages

- Happy grams

- Two-way, home-school notebooks

- Home-school contracts

- Class newsletters and websites

C. Telephone calls

- Short, positive calls from the teacher _____

_____

VI. Other Forms of Parent Involvement

- Parents as Teachers

- Parent Education and Support Groups

- Parent to Parent Groups

- Parents as Research Partners

VII. Current Issues and Future Trends

- Professionals who work with parents should _____

_____

- Family-centered services are predicated on the belief that the child is part of the family system and

_____

_____

_____

- Effective change for the child cannot be achieved without _____

_____

- A strength-based approach to family supports assumes that all families have_____

_____

_____

Homework

Write a 2- to 3-page paper on one of the following topics.

1. What are the greatest challenges for parents of children with disabilities? The many roles of parents of exceptional children are discussed in Chapter 3. The roles include caregiver, provider, teacher, counselor, behavior management specialist, parent of other siblings, marriage partner, information specialist/trainer for significant others, and advocate for school and community services. Discuss how the roles and challenges facing parents of children with disabilities differ from the roles and challenges of parents with nondisabled children. Discuss the greatest challenges of parents of exceptional children and how those challenges change as the children progress through each developmental stage (from infancy through adulthood).

2. See the Teaching & Learning module on the Companion Website for "A Parent-Professional Partnership in Positive Behavioral Support," which describes how a parent-professional partnership was used to systematically find meaningful solutions to a student's behavior problems. How can partnerships between parents and professionals be strengthened?

Group Project: Develop a Collaborative Multicultural Unit

Team up with 4 other students in your class to create a multicultural thematic unit.
1. Select a grade level for which you will be developing the unit.
2. Select a few instructional objectives for each skill and/or content area your group will be addressing in the unit (e.g., math, language arts, science, social studies, physical education, art, music).
3. Select a cultural group around which you will be planning the unit.
4. Each member of the group will select a skill or content area for which he or she will be responsible.
5. Gather information and materials about the cultural group your team has decided to study, and create 3 to 5 lesson plans for your designated skill/content area. For example, if the team is studying Chinese culture, the person responsible for the math skill area may develop problem-solving lessons using tangrams or magic squares.
6. Present your multicultural unit to the class.

CD-ROM Questions

1. What makes a good parent-teacher partnership?

   School: Dunkirk Elementary School
   Videos and Commentaries: IEP Meeting & Parent Teacher conferences

2. Describe potential barriers to parent-teacher communication. How might teachers overcome these barriers?

   School: Dunkirk Elementary School
   Videos and Commentaries: IEP Meeting & Parent Teacher conferences

3. How can a teacher achieve a positive classroom climate?

   School: Dunkirk Elementary School
   Videos and Commentaries: Mrs. Crangle, Mrs. Maheady, & Classroom Climate

Self-Check Quiz _____

1. A passive listener may attend to the content of what is said but doesn't interpret it in the context of who said it and how he said it.

2. Providing information is the first step in conducting a parent-teacher conference.

3. Parents have been the primary advocacy force for the education of children with disabilities.

4. Teachers can rely on written messages as the sole form of communication with parents.

5. The roles of behavior support specialist, counselor, and even teacher are typical ones taken on by parents of children with disabilities.

6. Parents prefer teachers who use technical jargon during a parent-teacher meeting.

7. One positive effect of mandating parent involvement in special education is that parents no longer need to fulfill the role of advocate.

8. The mirror model for parent involvement assumes that not all parents need all that professionals have to offer and that no parent should be expected to provide everything.

9. The process of becoming a culturally proficient teacher begins with gaining knowledge about other cultures.

10. Respite care refers to the temporary care of an individual with disabilities by nonfamily members.

11. Research and practice have shown that educational effectiveness is enhanced when parents and families are involved.

12. Children with disabilities are more likely to be reported in abuse and neglect cases, relative to children without disabilities.

13. IDEA requires collaboration between teachers and families.

14. Parents prefer teachers to contact them only when a problem arises.

15. Educators should use open-ended questions as much as possible when communicating with parents.

Essay Questions

1. Describe the basic principles of effective communication, providing an example for each principle cited.

2. Describe the steps for building cultural reciprocity, providing an example for each step.

CHAPTER FOUR
MENTAL RETARDATION

*Focus Questions*_____

- **What is most important in determining a person's level of adaptive functioning: intellectual capability or a supportive environment?**

  In many respects this is a trick question. Both intellectual capability and a supportive environment are important factors in the level of adaptive functioning of a person with MR. However; it is imperative that teachers and other support providers not have low expectations for the person who is mentally retarded. With the correct level of support, many people with MR are able to lead productive lives and achieve things many thought not possible.

- **What is to be gained by classifying a child with mental retardation according to the intensities of supports she needs to access and benefit from education?**

  The AAMR's "2002 System" provides recommendations for functionally classifying mental retardation according to needed supports. This approach is much more useful for planning and delivering appropriate special education services than classifying mental retardation by intellectual functioning. Needed supports are identified and classified by an interdisciplinary team according to four levels of intensities: intermittent, limited, extensive, and pervasive. This system reflects the idea that expression of the impairments is strongly affected by the life arrangements of the individual.

- **What should curriculum goals for students with mental retardation emphasize?**

  Not all students labeled mentally retarded have the same abilities or interests. Each student's program should be designed to fit his or her unique needs. Today, there are many different educational and residential placement options available. In general, however, functional skills that will lead to the child's independence in the community and workplace should be the focus of most educational programs for individuals with mental retardation.

- **What are the most important features of effective instruction for students with mental retardation?**

  There are six features to effective teaching which are based on the scientific method: (a) precise definition and task analysis of the new skill to be learned; (b) direct and frequent measurement of the student's performance; (c) frequent opportunities for active student responding; (d) immediate and systematic feedback; (e) procedures for achieving the transfer of stimulus control from instructional cues or prompts to naturally occurring stimuli; and (f) strategies for promoting the generalization and maintenance of newly learned skills to different, nontraining situations and environments.

- **What is necessary to make education for a student with mental retardation appropriate in an inclusive classroom?**

  Simply placing a child with disabilities into a regular classroom does not guarantee that the student will be accepted socially or receive the most appropriate and needed instructional programming. Factors that may determine the success of an inclusive placement in a regular classroom include: the child's level of functioning, the teacher's ability to individualize instruction and make appropriate accommodations, the degree of support and collaboration with other professionals, the extent of parent involvement, and the level of peer maturity.

Essential Concepts

- Mental retardation is a complex concept that is difficult to define. It involves significant deficits in both intellectual functioning and adaptive behavior—both of which are difficult to measure. Even the slightest rewording in the definition can influence who is considered mentally retarded and consequently who is eligible for special education services. The most recent definition of mental retardation moves away from deficits within the individual toward levels of support needed in the environment for the individual to function effectively.

- Effective instructional methodologies for these students include the use of a task analysis to target skills to be taught, direct and frequent measurement of learner's performance, instructional strategies that provide increased active student responding, use of systematic feedback, strategies for transferring stimulus control, and techniques for promoting generalization and maintenance of skills.

- Recent developments in instructional technology provide evidence that individuals with mental retardation can learn skills previously thought beyond their capability. Some children with mental retardation attend special public schools or live in institutional settings. More and more, however, are being educated in their neighborhood schools and are living in neighborhood settings where they make valuable contributions to their communities.

- Words such as *helpless, unteachable, dependent,* and *childlike* are often associated with people with mental retardation. Less often are people with mental retardation described with positive characteristics, such as *hardworking, capable, independent,* and *productive*. Yet many children and adults with mental retardation are just that: hard-working, capable, independent, and productive members of classrooms and communities. Some individuals with mental retardation, certainly, are not as capable as others, but this same statement can be made about any group of people.

Objectives

DEFINITIONS
1. List the components of the IDEA definition of *mental retardation*.
2. List the components of the AAMR's "new definition" of mental retardation.
3. List and describe the levels of needed support outlined in the "2002 system."

IDENTIFICATION AND ASSESSMENT
1. Describe the method for assessing intellectual functioning.
2. Describe the considerations when interpreting the results of IQ tests.
3. Define *adaptive behavior*.
4. Describe the method for assessing adaptive functioning.

PREVALENCE
1. Describe why estimating prevalence is difficult.

CAUSES AND PREVENTION
1. List and describe the biological causes of mental retardation.
2. Describe the environmental causes of mental retardation.
3. List the types of preventative measures.

CHARACTERISTICS OF STUDENTS WITH MENTAL RETARDATION
1. Describe the common characteristics of students with mild mental retardation.
2. Describe the common characteristics of students with moderate mental retardation.
3. Describe the common characteristics of students with severe mental retardation.

EDUCATIONAL APPROACHES
1. Identify and describe the curriculum goals for students with mental retardation.
2. Identify and describe effective instructional methods for students with mental retardation.

EDUCATIONAL PLACEMENT ALTERNATIVES
1. Describe the continuum of educational placements for students with mental retardation.

CURRENT ISSUES AND FUTURE TRENDS
1. Discuss issues confronting the field of mental retardation.

Chapter Four at a Glance

Main Topics	Key Points	Key Terms
Mental Retardation		
Definitions	The AAMR 1983 definition of mental retardation includes the following criteria: significantly subaverage intellectual functioning, deficits in adaptive behavior, and manifestation during the developmental period.	mild retardation moderate retardation severe retardation profound retardation intermittent support limited support extensive support pervasive support adaptive behavior
	AAMR's new definition based on needed supports states that students with MR have significant limitations in both intellectual functioning and conceptual, social, and practical adaptive skills, and the disability originates before age 18.	
	Classification of MR according to AAMR's 1992/2002 definition is based on four levels of support: intermittent, limited, extensive, and pervasive.	
Identification and Assessment	Norm-referenced, standardized IQ tests, such as the Wechsler Intelligence Scale for Children—Third Edition and the Stanford-Binet IV, are used to assess intelligence.	standardized test norm-referenced test normal curve standard deviation adaptive behavior scales
	A diagnosis of MR requires an IQ score at least 2 standard deviations below the mean (70 or less).	
	Although IQ scores have proven to be the single best predictor of school achievement, they have some important limitations.	
	Adaptive behavior is the effectiveness or degree with which the individual meets the standards of personal independence and social responsibility expected of his age and social group.	
	The AAMR Adaptive Behavior Scale and Vineland Adaptive Behavior Scales are commonly used to assess adaptive behavior.	
	Measurement of adaptive behavior has proven difficult because of the relative nature of social adjustment and competence.	
Characteristics	Most students with mild MR master academic skills up to about sixth grade and are able to learn job skills well enough to support themselves independently or semi-independently.	generalization behavioral excesses
	People with moderate MR are more likely to have physical disabilities and behavior problems than are individuals with mild MR.	
	Almost always identified at birth or shortly after, most students with severe MR have significant central nervous system damage and additional disabilities or health conditions.	

Chapter Four at a Glance

Main Topics	Key Points	Key Terms
Characteristics (continued)	Students with mental retardation have poor memory, slower rates of learning, poor generalization, and difficulty with higher-order cognitive skills, and may exhibit poor motivation.	
	Adaptive behavior deficits tend to occur across the following domains of functioning: self-care and daily living skills, social development, and behavioral excesses.	
Prevalence	During the 1999–2000 school year, approximately 1% of the total school enrollment received special education services in the MR category.	
Causes and Prevention	More than 250 causes of MR have been identified.	prenatal perinatal postnatal psychosocial disadvantage developmental retardation amniocentesis chorion villus sampling
	Causes are categorized by the terms *prenatal* (e.g., chromosomal disorders, syndrome disorders), *perinatal* (e.g., intrauterine disorders, neonatal disorders), and *postnatal* (e.g., head injuries, infections, degenerative disorders, malnutrition).	
	When there is no biological evidence, the cause is presumed to be psychosocial disadvantage. Deprivation in the early years of life is the key cause of environmentally caused MR.	
Educational Approaches	A functional curriculum will maximize a student's independence, self-direction, and enjoyment in everyday school, home, community, and work environments.	functional curriculum life skills self-determination applied behavior analysis task analysis active student response positive reinforcement acquisition stage of learning practice stage of learning stimulus control
	Skills that will help students with MR transition into adult life in the community include a functional curriculum, life skills, and self-determination.	
	The principles of applied behavior analysis (e.g., task analysis, direct and frequent measurement, active student responding, systematic feedback) provide effective strategies for teaching students with MR.	
Educational Placement Alternatives	Although some children with MR attend special schools, most are educated in their neighborhood schools (special classes, regular class with support, or resource room).	inclusion
	The extent to which a student with MR should be included in the regular classroom should be determined by the student's individual needs.	
Current Issues and Future Trends	Two issues confronting the field of MR are a continued search for a definition and increasing the acceptance and membership of persons with MR in society.	
	An especially important and continuing challenge is moving beyond the physical integration of persons with MR in society to acceptance and membership that comes from holding valued roles.	

Guided Review

I. Definitions

   A. Definition in IDEA

- Significantly subaverage _____

- Deficits in _____

- Manifested during the _____

   B. AAMR's Definition Based on Needed Supports

- Provides conceptual and procedural recommendations for functionally classifying mental

  retardation according_____

- Intensities of supports: _____

II. Identification and Assessment

   A. Assessing Intellectual Functioning

- Norm-referenced, standardized IQ tests are used to assess _____

- A diagnosis of MR requires an IQ score of at least _____

- IQ scores have proven to be the single best predictor of _____

- Important considerations of IQ tests:

  1. IQ is a _____

  2. IQ tests measure how a child performs _____

  3. IQ tests can be _____

  4. IQ scores can _____

  5. IQ testing is not _____

  6. Results should never be used as the sole basis for _____

  _____

  _____

  7. Results from an IQ test should not be used to _____

   B. Assessing Adaptive Behavior

- Adaptive behavior is the collection of conceptual, social, and practical skills that have been learned by people in order to _____

- Instruments used to assess adaptive behavior include: _____

_____

- Measurement of adaptive behavior has proven difficult because of the _____

_____

III. Characteristics

- Many children with mild MR are not identified until they _____, can master skills

up to about _____, and are able to learn job skills well enough to _____

- Children with moderate MR show significant developmental delays in their _____.

- They are more likely to have _____ than students with mild MR.

- Individuals with severe/profound MR are almost always identified _____

- Most have significant _____, additional disabilities, and health
conditions.

A. Cognitive Functioning

- Students with mental retardation have: _____

_____

B. Adaptive Behavior

- Adaptive behavior deficits tend to occur across the following domains of functioning: _____

_____

_____

C. Positive Attributes

- Individuals with mental retardation are a huge and disparate group composed of people with
highly individual personalities.

IV. Prevalence

- Approximately 1% of the total school enrollment received special education services in the MR
category.

V. Causes and Prevention

A. Causes

- More than _____ causes of MR have been identified.

- Etiological factors are categorized as _____

- For about 50% of mild MR cases and 30% of severe MR cases, the cause is _____

B. Biological Causes

- Specific biological causes are identified for about _____

    _____

- The term syndrome refers to a number of symptoms or characteristics that occur together and

    provide the_____

C. Environmental Causes

- Mild MR cases make up about _____ of all persons with MR.

- In the vast majority of those cases, there is no evidence of _____

- When there is no biological evidence, the cause is presumed to be _____

- Deprivation in the early years of life is the key cause of environmentally caused MR.

D. Prevention

- The biggest single preventative strike against MR was the development of _____

- Advances in medical science have enabled doctors to identify certain _____

- Amniocentesis and chorion villus sampling can confirm _____

- Toxic exposure through _____ are two major
    causes of preventable MR

- Most mild MR is thought to be the result of an _____ during the
    early years.

VI. Educational Approaches

A. Curriculum Goals

- A functional curriculum will maximize a student's _____

    _____

- Life skills will help students with MR transition into _____

- Self-determined learners set goals, plan and implement a course of action, _____

    _____

B. Instructional Methods

- Students with MR learn best when instruction is _____

- Task analysis is breaking down _____

  _____

- Teachers should verify the effects of their instruction through _____

- Active student responding results in _____

  _____

- Systematic feedback is generally more effective when it is _____

  _____

- Response prompts should be gradually and _____

- Generalization and Maintenance

  1. Aiming for natural contingencies of reinforcement means teaching skills that will be

     _____

  2. Programming common stimuli means making the teaching environment as similar as

     possible to the _____

  3. Community-based instruction increases the probability of _____

     _____

VII. Educational Placement Alternatives

- Approximately 50% of students with MR are educated in _____,

  30% in *resource rooms*, and 15% in _____.

- During the early elementary years, many students with MR benefit from _____

  _____

VIII. Current Issues and Future Trends

- Changes and debate over the definition of mental retardation are likely to continue

- The principles of normalization, social role valorization, and self-determination are important in helping individuals with MR achieve acceptance and membership in society.

Homework

Write a 2- to 3-page paper on one of the following topics.

1. *The Mismeasure of Man* (1996) by Stephan J. Gould provides a cogent critique of the use of IQ tests. Among his criticisms is the tendency for "reification" or converting abstract concepts (like IQ) into measurable objects. Write a 2-page reaction paper to the following quote in the book:

   > The principle error, in fact, has involved a major theme of this book: reification—in this case, the notion that such a nebulous, socially defined concept as intelligence might be identified as a "thing" with a locus in the brain and a definite degree of heritability—and that it might be measured as a single number, thus permitting a unilinear ranking of people according to the amount of it they possess. (pp. 268–269).

   Respond to the following questions in your paper.
   - Define *intelligence* in your own words.
   - Can something like intelligence be measured?
   - Cultural background has been shown to affect the results of intelligence tests. What does this say about the validity of intelligence as a real entity?
   - What are the advantages and disadvantages of using intelligence tests for placing students?

2. Can a functional curriculum be taught effectively in inclusive classrooms? Identifying functional curriculum goals and objectives for children with mental retardation has become a priority in special education. A functional curriculum should maximize a student's independence, self-direction, and enjoyment in school, home, community, and work environments. Write a 3- to 4-page position paper discussing the extent to which functional curriculum goals can be met in an inclusive regular education classroom. Under what circumstances should resource or self-contained classrooms be the placement option for instruction of functional skills?

CD-ROM Questions

1. Identify as many examples as you can of the characteristics in Ms. Trask-Tyler's classroom that help make it an effective, efficient, and inviting environment for students and teachers.

   School: Blendon Middle School
   Video and Commentaries: Ms. Trask-Tyler

2. Describe a classroom or school activity (that is not shown in a video) to teach functional living skills to students with moderate or intensive disabilities.

   School: Blendon Middle School
   Videos and Commentaries: Vocational Skills, Functional Curriculum, Service Learning, & Class Auction

3. Suppose you would like to teach a student with mental retardation to make microwave popcorn. Outline the steps involved in teaching this skill and describe how you might embed academic skill instruction (e.g., reading, math) into the lesson.

   School: Blendon Middle School
   Videos and Commentaries: Functional Curriculum & Class Auction

4. Why is direct and frequent assessment of student learning important?

    School: Como Elementary School
    Videos and Commentaries: Test Group

Self-Check Quiz

True/False

1. Joyce is a teacher. After suffering a head injury in a car accident, she has subaverage intellectual functioning and adaptive behavior deficits. She will probably not be diagnosed as mentally retarded.

2. Much of the variability in the prevalence rates of mental retardation is explained by socioeconomic status.

3. Because students with mental retardation learn at a slower rate, teachers should always provide plenty of time for them to complete their work.

4. The classifications of educable mentally retarded (EMR) and trainable mentally retarded (TMR) are favored because they help teachers define achievement limits.

5. The vast majority of people with mental retardation have mild retardation and no apparent neurological or biological pathology.

6. If a traditional academic skill is not a typical activity or learning outcome for students with mental retardation, teachers should assume that it is not functional.

7. Time trials should be used only after students have learned how to do a skill correctly.

8. AAMR's 2002 definition of mental retardation emphasizes the importance of inclusive educational placements.

9. Teaching students with mental retardation to seek teacher attention and assistance when they want help is a way of fostering independence.

10. A child with Down syndrome has an IQ around the 1st percentile but becomes a television personality, demonstrating near-average functioning in the community. He probably would not be classified as mentally retarded.

11. Students in the practice stage of learning should be given feedback after every response to assure that errors are not practiced.

12. AAMR's new definition of mental retardation is the basis for radical change in state guidelines for identification.

13. Most cases of mild mental retardation are believed to be caused by factors that occur before or during birth.

14. Inclusion for children with mental retardation is most beneficial if it is provided in the secondary years, as a prelude to transition.

15. Intelligence test scores highly correlate with academic achievement.

Essay Questions

1. Describe the intent of curriculum goals for individuals with mental retardation, providing five examples of such goals for a fictitious child.

2. Describe normalization and the related concept of social role valorization.

CHAPTER FIVE
LEARNING DISABILITIES

Focus Questions _____

- **Why has the concept of learning disabilities proven so difficult to define?**

There are many different kinds of academic and social skills that students are expected to learn during their formal education. In addition, there is a wide range of individual differences among learners in any given classroom. Thus, no large group of children can be expected to learn the same skill at exactly the same rate or to the exact same level of proficiency. So, in one sense, all students could be said to be learning disabled in relation to some level of "standard" performance. Primarily for these reasons (among others), experts in the field of learning disabilities have struggled to provide a coherent definition that excludes those who should be excluded and includes those who should be included. Moreover, the definition itself provides the classroom teacher with little useful information about how or what to teach a particular student. Therefore, the majority of educational professionals' efforts should be devoted to the development and delivery of effective instruction rather than debates over definitions.

- **Do most students who are identified as learning disabled have a true disability? Or are they just low achievers or victims of poor instruction?**

They are probably both. Learning disabilities are considered by some to be a school-defined phenomenon because the disability is most commonly exhibited through difficulties in mastering academic skills. However, the process of learning how to read or do mathematics is not fundamentally different from learning how to drive a car, operate a computer, drive a nail, or make a friend. While learning disabilities are often specific to certain kinds of skills, many individuals have difficulty learning across a wide range of settings and situations. The student who has experienced difficulties in learning throughout school will not magically lose this disability upon graduation. The learning disability will change only in the sense that the skills to be learned are different.

- **What are the most important skills for an elementary-age student with learning disabilities to master? For a secondary student with disabilities?**

Instruction must continuously change to meet the changing needs of the student. As students with learning disabilities get older, different teaching settings and/or instructional priorities may be warranted. For example, instruction may need to focus less on basic skills and concentrate more on such skills as learning strategies and self-management techniques. The most important skills are those that meet the needs of the student at each level of their academic and social development.

- **How do basic academic skills and learning strategies relate to each other?**

Learning strategies are procedures a student follows when planning, executing, and evaluating performance on a task and its outcomes. In order to become proficient in the use of learning strategies, students will need at least some knowledge of and proficiency at applying basic academic skills.

- **Should all students with learning disabilities be educated in the regular classroom?**

For the majority of students with LD, the least restrictive environment is the regular classroom for all or most of the day. The movement towards full inclusion has many advocates for students with LD worried. Although the full-inclusion movement has the best intentions for children with disabilities, little research supports it. Most special educators believe that the placement of students with disabilities should be determined on an individual basis.

Essential Concepts _____

- Learning disabilities are often called "invisible disabilities" because there are no physical signs associated with the diagnosis, yet ironically, it is by far the largest IDEA category in terms of children served in special education.

- There is no standard, universally accepted definition of what constitutes a learning disability. However, the fundamental, defining characteristic of students with learning disabilities is: specific and significant achievement discrepancy in the presence of adequate overall intelligence.

- The causes of a specified learning disability are often unknown. Nevertheless children with LD frequently display reading problems, deficits in written language, academic underachievement, and social skills problems, and are sometimes inattentive and hyperactive.

- Assessment is essential to planning an instructional program to teach the skills a child needs to acquire. Using assessment information to improve instruction is at the heart of "best practice" in educating students with learning disabilities. Educational approaches should focus on the child's specific skill deficit. Approaches such as curriculum-based measurement, precision teaching, explicit instruction, content enhancement, and learning strategies have been empirically supported as effective teaching strategies for students with LD.

- All children have difficulty learning at one time or another or to one degree or another. In addition, most students with LD spend at least part of the day in the general education classroom. Therefore, an understanding of LD is important for all teachers, because they are likely to meet children with some type of learning problem in their own classroom one day.

Objectives _____

DEFINITIONS
1. List the components of the federal (IDEA) definition of LD.
2. List the components of the proposed NJCLD definition of LD.
3. Compare (similarities) and contrast (differences) the two definitions.
4. List the three criteria that most states use to identify children with LD.

CHARACTERISTICS
1. Describe the academic and social skills deficits associated with LD.
2. Identify the "defining characteristic" of children with LD.

PREVALENCE
1. List the prevalence estimates for children with LD.

CAUSES
1. Describe the four hypothesized causes of LD.
2. List the three reasons why educators should not place too much emphasis on theories linking LD with brain dysfunction.

ASSESSMENT
1. Compare and contrast the various types of assessment for LD.
2. Discuss the advantages of direct daily measurement.

EDUCATIONAL APPROACHES
1. Define and describe the major principles of effective instructional design.
2. List the characteristics of explicit instruction.

3. Provide examples of content enhancements for children with LD.
4. Provide examples of learning strategies for children with LD.

EDUCATIONAL PLACEMENT ALTERNATIVES
1. Identify and describe the various placement alternatives for students with LD.

CURRENT ISSUES AND FUTURE TRENDS
1. Discuss the two issues concerning the continuing debate over defining LD.
2. Discuss the need for the continuum of services for children with LD.
3. Describe the reasons for maintaining a positive focus when educating children with LD.

Chapter Five at a Glance

Main Topics	Key Points	Key Terms
Learning Disabilities	In IDEA, a learning disability is defined as a disorder in one or more of the basic psychological processes. It does not include learning problems that are the result of visual, hearing, or motor disabilities; mental retardation; emotional disturbance; or an environmental disadvantage.	
Definitions	Although there is no universally agreed-on definition of learning disabilities, most states and school districts require that three criteria be met to qualify for special education services: (1) a severe discrepancy between ability and achievement, (2) learning problems cannot be attributed to other disabilities, and (3) a need for special education services.	
Characteristics	Students with learning disabilities experience one or more of the following characteristics: reading problems, deficits in written language, underachievement in math, poor social skills, attention deficits and hyperactivity, and behavioral problems.	minimal brain dysfunction dyslexia
	Specific and significant achievement deficits in the presence of adequate overall intelligence are the defining characteristics of a learning disability.	
Prevalence	Learning disabilities is by far the largest of all special education categories. About half of all children receiving special education services are identified as having LD.	
	Students with LD represent about 5% of the school-age population.	
Causes	In most cases of learning disabilities, there is no known cause. Four suspected causes are brain damage or dysfunction, heredity, biochemical imbalance, and environmental factors.	biochemical imbalance
	Assuming a child's learning problems are caused by a dysfunctioning brain can serve as a built-in excuse for ineffective instruction.	
	There is growing evidence that genetics may account for at least some family links with dyslexia.	
	Today, most professionals in learning disabilities give little credence to biochemical imbalance as a significant cause of learning problems.	
	Impoverished living conditions early in a child's life and poor instruction probably contribute to the achievement deficits in the LD category.	
Assessment	Intelligence and achievement tests are administered to determine if there is a discrepancy between intellectual ability and achievement. Other forms of assessment are criterion-referenced tests, informal reading inventories, and direct daily measurement.	norm-referenced tests criterion-referenced tests curriculum-based assessment precision teaching

Chapter Five at a Glance

Main Topics	Key Points	Key Terms
Educational Approaches	Research has shown that students with learning disabilities have difficulty organizing information on their own, bring limited stores of background knowledge to many academic activities, and often do not approach learning tasks in effective and efficient ways.	explicit instruction content enhancements guided notes learning strategies mnemonic device
	Many students' learning problems can be remediated by direct, intensive, and systematic instruction.	
	Content enhancement is the general name given to a wide range of techniques that teachers use to enhance the delivery of critical curriculum content so that students are better able to organize, comprehend, and retain the information. Examples of content enhancements are guided notes, graphic organizers and visual displays, and mnemonics.	
	Learning strategies help students guide themselves successfully through specific tasks or general problems.	
Educational Placement Alternatives	During the 1998–1999 school year, 43% of students with learning disabilities were educated in regular classrooms.	consultant teacher resource room
	Some school districts employ a collaborative teaching model to support the full inclusion of students with learning disabilities.	
	A consultant teacher provides support to regular classroom teachers and other school staff who work directly with students with learning disabilities. The consultant teacher helps the regular teacher select assessment devices, curriculum materials, and instructional activities.	
	A resource room is a specially staffed and equipped classroom where students with learning disabilities come for one or several periods during the school day to received individualized instruction.	
Current Issues and Future Trends	The discussion and debate over what constitutes a true learning disability are likely to continue.	
	It is important for schools to respond to the individual needs of all children with disabilities.	
	Most professionals and advocates for students with learning disabilities do not support full inclusion, which would eliminate the continuum of service delivery options.	
	Students with learning disabilities possess positive attributes and interests that teachers should identify and try to strengthen.	

Guided Review _____

I. Definitions

- In IDEA, a learning disability is defined as a disorder in _____

    _____

- It does not include learning problems that are the result of _____

    _____

- The NJCLD definition addresses the weaknesses of the IDEA definition.

- Most states and school districts require that three criteria be met: _____

    _____

II. Characteristics

- Students with learning disabilities display one or more of the following characteristics: _____

    _____

    _____

- The defining characteristic of LD: _____

    _____

III. Prevalence

- Learning disabilities is by far the largest of all special education categories.

- Half of all children with disabilities receive services under the LD category.

- Five out of every 100 students in the United States have LD.

IV. Causes

- In most cases, the cause of LD is _____

    A. Brain Damage or Dysfunction

    - In most cases of LD, there is no evidence of brain damage or dysfunction.

    - Assuming a child's learning problems are caused by brain dysfunction can serve as a _____

        _____

    B. Heredity

    - There is growing evidence that genetics may account for _____

C. Biochemical Imbalance

- Today, most professionals in learning disabilities give little credence to biochemical imbalance as a _____

D. Environmental Factors

- Impoverished living conditions early in a child's life and poor instruction _____

    _____

- Many students' learning problems can be remediated by _____

    _____

V. Assessment

- Intelligence and achievement tests are administered to determine if there is a discrepancy between

    _____

- Other forms of assessment are _____

    _____

VI. Educational Approaches

- Research has shown that students with learning disabilities have difficulty _____

    _____

    _____

VII. Explicit Instruction

- Provide students with a _____

- Provide models of proficient performance

- Have students explain _____

- Provide frequent, positive _____

- Provide adequate _____

A. Content Enhancements

- *Content enhancement* is the general name given to a wide range of techniques that teachers use to enhance the delivery of critical curriculum content so students are better able _____

    _____

- Examples of content enhancements are_____

  _____

B. Learning Strategies

- Proficient learners approach tasks and problems _____

- Students use task-specific strategies to _____

  _____

- A mnemonic device might be used to help students remember _____

VIII. Educational Placement Alternatives

  A. Regular Classroom

  - IDEA requires that students with disabilities be educated with their nondisabled peers and

    have access to the core curriculum to the _____

  B. Consultant Teacher

  - A consultant teacher provides support to _____

  - The consultant teacher helps the regular teacher select_____

    _____

  C. Resource Room

  - A resource room is a specially staffed and equipped classroom where students with learning

    disabilities _____

  - Some advantages of the resource room are that _____

    _____

    _____

  - Some disadvantages are that _____

    _____

IX. Current Issues and Future Trends

  - Movement to redefine LD as_____

  - Continuing debates about the true nature of _____

  - Most professionals and advocates for students with LD do not support _____

Homework

Write a 2- to 3-page paper on one of the following topics.

1. Review the sections of this chapter on content enhancement and learning strategies. Write a lesson plan on a topic of your choice. Incorporate a variety of the strategies outlined in the chapter.

2. Develop a set of guided notes that would be used with a lesson on the content area and skill level of your choice. Refer to the suggestions for creating guided notes in Chapter 5.

3. The most common practice for identifying children with learning disabilities is determining if a discrepancy exists between their ability and achievement. The discrepancy criterion is usually determined by comparing the student's IQ score to an achievement test score. There are many problems with this system of identification. According to Sternberg and Grigorenko (2001), "We should immediately stop using discrepancy scores to identify children with learning disabilities. The method is psychologically and psychometrically indefensible. It must go."(p. 339). Write a paper explaining some of the problems with the discrepancy criterion, and suggest alternative ways of identifying children with learning disabilities.

CD-ROM Questions

1. Who benefits from the pair tutoring program?

   School: Dunkirk Middle School
   Video and Commentaries: Extra Tutoring

2. How might students with disabilities benefit from explicit instruction?

   School: Millennium Community School
   Videos and Commentaries: Direct Instruction & Clocklight Management

3. What are the advantages of choral responding?

   School: Millennium Community School
   Videos and Commentaries: Choral Responding, Direct Instruction, & Clocklight Management

4. What does "creativity with a purpose" mean to you? Give an example.

   School: Como Elementary School
   Videos and Commentaries: Tutoring Procedures

Self-Check Quiz

True/False

1. More children are identified as learning disabled than any other IDEA category.

2. A consultant teacher may work with many regular classroom teachers but may never actually work with students.

3. Ralph never attended school until age nine, so he is far behind his peers academically. Using IDEA criteria, it's still possible that he can be identified as learning disabled.

4. The fundamental, defining characteristic of learning disabilities is specific and significant achievement deficits in conjunction with adequate intelligence.

5. Many educators and experts contend that the ever-increasing number of children identified as learning disabled is from overidentification of low achievers.

6. The preferred treatment for children with attention-deficit/hyperactivity disorder is drug therapy.

7. Most students with learning disabilities have reading and math deficits but typical social skills.

8. Under IDEA, students with learning problems that result from an emotional disturbance cannot be identified as learning disabled.

9. Attention deficit/hyperactivity disorder is a learning disability.

10. Because of IDEA criteria, a child who is identified as learning disabled in one state would have also been identified if evaluated in another state.

11. All students with learning disabilities experience reading problems.

12. Ability-achievement discrepancy is typically measured by comparing a student's IQ score to an achievement test score to determine if they are consistent.

13. Mnemonics are increasingly used to help assess students with suspected learning disabilities.

14. Criterion-referenced tests, direct daily measurement, and curriculum-based measurement are all commonly used to assess suspected learning disabilities.

15. The primary instructional focus in educating children with learning disabilities is remediation.

Essay Questions

1. Describe the criticisms of the IDEA definition of learning disabilities that led the National Joint Committee on Learning Disabilities (NJCLD) to create their own definition.

2. Explain the importance of phonemic awareness, and provide four examples of behaviors that indicate that a child is phonemically aware.

CHAPTER SIX
EMOTIONAL AND BEHAVIORAL DISORDERS

Focus Questions

- **Why should a child who behaves badly be considered disabled?**

One of the most critical factors for determining our acceptance and success in school, work, and community is our behavior. The way we behave and interact with others has a direct influence on how well we learn. For example, a student who spends a large part of his day antagonizing other students, refusing to participate in class activities, and defying the teacher will probably not succeed academically. The adult who argues with co-workers, customers, and supervisors is likely to lose his or her job. Why then should children who behave badly be considered disabled? Their misconduct can interfere with their acceptance by others, their access to important opportunities, and the quality of their lives.

- **Who is more severely disabled: the acting-out, antisocial child, or the withdrawn child?**

When attempting to determine the relative severity of a disorder, it is necessary to examine the individual child and the extent to which the behavior interferes with his or her ability to function. Acting-out children tend to be disruptive. Their emotional and behavioral disorders interfere with their acquisition of important skills. Although withdrawn children may not be disruptive, their behavior also interferes with their learning. Acting-out and withdrawn children are probably equally disabled because both encounter problems with the acquisition of academic, social, personal, and vocational skills. From an identification perspective, withdrawn children may be more disabled because they are less likely to be identified and to receive treatment.

- **How are behavior problems and academic performance interrelated?**

There is a strong correlation between low academic achievement and behavior disorders. Behavior problems almost always lead to failure in academic performance, and a history of academic failure may predispose students to further antisocial behavior. For this reason, teachers of students with EBD must break this cycle by focusing on interventions that address both academic and behavior deficits. Improvement in behavior may create a situation more conducive to learning, while academic success may decrease behavior problems.

- **How can a teacher's efforts to defuse a classroom disturbance contribute to an escalation of misbehavior?**

Some teachers of students with EBD create an environment in which coercion is the primary means for controlling inappropriate behavior. Coercive environments promote escape and avoidance by those being coerced. Teachers of students with emotional and behavioral disorders must strive to design classroom environments that are effective for decreasing antisocial behavior and increasing the frequency of positive teacher-student interactions.

- **What are the most important skills for teachers of students with emotional and behavioral disorders?**

All teachers, including those who teach students with EBD, must be skilled in delivering effective instruction so that students will attain mastery of important academic and social skills. The most effective teachers will create positive, supportive environments that promote and maintain student success. Teachers of students with emotional and behavioral disorders must have good problem-solving skills and be prepared for the challenge of managing and changing disruptive behaviors.

Essential Concepts _____

- Rhode, Jenson, and Reavis (1999) describe children with emotional and behavioral problems as "tough kids." Perhaps no other label describes them so well. Many of them have few friends, and they often behave in such a persistently obnoxious manner that they seem to invite negative responses from peers and adults. However, anyone who has ever taught "tough kids" will tell you that they can be bright, creative, energetic, and even fun to be around under the right circumstances.

- This chapter begins with a discussion of the federal (IDEA) and alternate (CCBD) definitions of emotional and behavioral disorders. Although the IDEA definition provides the foundation for receiving specialized services, there are many troubling aspects of the definition, not the least of which is that the definition disqualifies many of the children that would benefit from special education. In response, the Council for Children with Behavior Disorders (CCBD) proposed an alternate definition of emotional and behavioral disorders as a disability characterized by "behavioral or emotional responses in school programs so different from appropriate age, cultural, or ethnic norms that they adversely affect educational performance."

- Boys are as much as four times more likely to be given the label of EBD than girls. Most children with EBD exhibit externalizing behaviors (e.g., noncompliance, aggression, tantrums), but many exhibit internalizing behaviors (e.g., excessive shyness, depression). Because children who manifest internalizing behaviors may be less disturbing to others than children who emit externalizing behaviors, they are in danger of underidentification.

- The causes of EBD are poorly understood, and estimates of the number of children with EBD vary widely. Nevertheless, explanations for the causes of EBD generally tend to fall into two categories, biological or environmental. Biological factors may include heredity and temperament. Environmental factors include home, community, peers, and school.

- Identification and assessment should be conducted as early as possible. Most screening devices usually consist of behavioral rating scales and teacher checklists. However, with the renewal of IDEA (1997), increased emphasis has been placed on direct measurement of behavior as exemplified by functional behavioral assessment (FBA).

- In order for children with EBD to become productive members of society, curriculum and instruction must focus primarily on academics and self-management skills. Research indicates that improving academic performance also has collateral effects on social skills. However, improvements in social skills do not usually correlate with improved academic performance. Whatever the focus, teachers should remember to concentrate on alterable variables, aspects of the environment that make a difference in the student's life and can be affected by teaching practices.

- Effective teaching practices for students with EBD include a positive, proactive approach to classroom management; clear rules and behavioral expectations; the systematic use of teacher praise; and high levels of active student responding (ASR). Recent efforts aimed at schoolwide positive behavioral support may also help to remediate many behavioral problems.

Objectives

DEFINITIONS
1. List the components of the federal (IDEA) definition of emotional disturbance.
2. List the components of the proposed (CCBD) definition of emotional and behavioral disorders.
3. Compare (similarities) and contrast (differences) the two definitions.
4. Describe the problems with both the federal and proposed definition.

CHARACTERISTICS
1. Define and provide examples of externalizing behaviors.
2. Define and provide examples of internalizing behaviors.
3. Describe the academic and social prognosis of children with EBD.

PREVALENCE
1. List the prevalence figures for children with EBD.
2. In relation to the definition of EBD, discuss why prevalence data are difficult to determine and their impact on children in need of specialized services.

CAUSES
1. Identify and provide examples of the two likely causes of EBD.
2. Describe the factors that place a student at risk for being identified with EBD.

IDENTIFICATION AND ASSESSMENT
1. Compare and contrast the various types of assessment for EBD.
2. Define and provide examples of five measurable dimensions of behavior.
3. Discuss the advantages of assessment based on direct observation of measurable behavior.
4. Describe the process of functional behavioral assessment.

EDUCATIONAL APPROACHES
1. Discuss the curriculum goals for children with EBD.
2. Discuss the importance of reinforcement-based, proactive classroom management strategies.
3. Describe the components of a schoolwide system of positive behavioral support.
4. Discuss the importance of teaching self-management skills.
5. Define and describe peer-mediated support.
6. Define and describe alterable variables in relation to teaching students with EBD.
7. Describe the affective traits of good teachers.

EDUCATIONAL PLACEMENT ALTERNATIVES
1. Describe the continuum of educational placements for students with EBD.

CURRENT ISSUES AND FUTURE TRENDS
1. Discuss five problem areas for providing effective, appropriate educational services for students with EBD.

Chapter Six at a Glance

Main Topics	Key Points	Key Terms
Emotional and Behavioral Disorders Definitions	The IDEA definition identifies the following conditions for a student to qualify for special education services: severity, chronicity, and difficulty in school. The CCBD definition clarifies the educational dimensions of the disability, focuses direction on behavior in school settings, and places behavior in the context of ethnic and cultural norms.	chronicity severity
Characteristics	The most common pattern of children with EBD is externalizing behaviors such as aggression and noncompliance. A pattern of antisocial behavior early in a child's development is the best single predictor of delinquency in adolescence. Children with internalizing behavior disorders have too little social interaction and tend to be withdrawn and depressed. Children with internalizing behavior disorders (withdrawn, depressed, anxious) are in more danger of not being identified. Most students with EBD perform academically at least one or more years below grade level, and they perform in the slow learner range on IQ tests (mean = 86).	externalizing behavior internalizing behavior
Prevalence	Estimates of the number of students with EBD vary widely (from 1% to 10%). Far fewer children with EBD are receiving special education services than the most conservative prevalence estimates.	delinquent recidivist
Causes	Theories and conceptual models of EBD include biological factors (brain disorders, genetics, temperament) and environmental factors (home, community, school).	brain dygenesis temperament coercive pain control
Identification and Assessment	Children with suspected EBD can be evaluated using screening tests, projective tests, and/or direct observation and measurement of behavior. Behavior can be measured objectively along the following dimensions: rate, magnitude, duration, latency, and topography. Functional behavioral assessment examines behavior in the context of antecedent and consequent events for the purpose of designing interventions.	projective tests latency topography functional behavioral assessment functional analysis

Chapter Six at a Glance

Main Topics	Key Points	Key Terms
Educational Approaches	The curriculum for students with EBD includes instruction in both academic and social skills. Behavior management interventions include discipline and schoolwide systems of behavior support, classroom management, self-management, and peer mediation. Teachers must possess differential acceptance and an empathetic relationship to deal effectively with students with EBD. Special educators must focus their efforts on those aspects of the student's life they can effectively control (alterable variables).	proactive strategies shaping contingency contracting extinction differential reinforcement response cost time out self-monitoring self-evaluation differential acceptance empathetic relationship alterable variables
Educational Placement Alternatives	Students with EBD typically receive special education services in self-contained or resource classrooms. Nearly half of all students with EBD spend at least part of the school day in regular classrooms. Most students receiving special education because of EBD have serious problems that require intensive interventions in highly structured environments.	
Current Issues and Future Trends	All students with severe behavior problems need to be eligible to receive special education services. Efforts to prevent EBD need to be increased through early screening, identification, and intervention. It is necessary to develop valid and reliable methods for conducting manifestation determinations required by IDEA disciplinary provisions. Services for youth in juvenile corrections systems need to be improved. Wraparound systems of comprehensive care can increase the likelihood that students with EBD will have their needs met. The most effective wraparound programs are characterized by child- and family-centered interventions and supports, interagency cooperation, and individualized care.	manifestation determination wraparound services

Guided Review

I. Definitions: a clear definition of behavioral disorders is lacking for the following reasons:

- Disordered behavior is a social _____

- Concepts and terminology used across theories can be inconsistent.

- There are different expectations for appropriate behavior across_____

- Emotional problems sometimes occur in conjunction with _____

  A. IDEA Definition of Emotional Disturbance

  - _____: over a long period of time

  - _____: to a marked degree

  - _____: adversely affects educational performance

  B. CCBD Definition of Emotional or Behavioral Disorders

  - Behavioral or emotional responses so different from appropriate age, cultural, or ethnic norms that they adversely affect educational performance; co-exist with other disabilities; include sustained disorders of conduct or adjustment affecting educational performance.

  - This definition clarifies the educational dimensions of the disability,

    focuses directly on _____,

    places behavior in the context of appropriate _____,

    increases the possibility of _____,

    and does not require distinctions between _____

II. Characteristics

  A. Externalizing Behaviors

  - Examples of externalizing behaviors: _____

  - _____ is the "king-pin behavior" around which other behavioral excesses evolve.

  - A pattern of antisocial behavior early in a child's development is the best single predictor of

    _____

B. Internalizing Behaviors: too little social interaction with others

- Examples of internalizing behaviors: _____

- Without identification and effective treatment, the extreme emotional disorders of some children can lead to _____

C. Academic Achievement

- Most students with EBD perform at least one or more years below their grade level and exhibit significant deficiencies in _____

- There is a strong correlation between _____

D. Intelligence

- Many children with EBD score in the _____ on IQ tests.

- It is almost certain that the disturbed child's inappropriate behavior has interfered with _____

  _____

E. Social Skills and Interpersonal Relationships

- Students with EBD reported lower levels of empathy toward others, participation in fewer curricular activities, less frequent contact with friends, and lower-quality relationships than were reported by their peers without disabilities.

III. Prevalence

- Between 1% and 7% of students have chronic problems with behavior that require_____

  _____

- Such varying estimates suggest that_____

- Although EBD ranked as the fourth-largest disability category in special education, most children with EBD _____

A. Gender

- The vast majority of children identified for special education because of EBD are _____

B. Juvenile Delinquency

- Juveniles, who comprise about 20% of the total population, were involved in 16% of all violent crimes and 32% of all property crime arrests in 1999.

- About half of all juvenile delinquents are _____

IV. Causes

    A. Biological Factors

- Brain disorders: For the vast majority of children with EBD,_____
  _____

- Genetics: evidence of genetic link for_____

- Temperament: may predispose a child to behavior problems

    B. Environmental Factors

- Three primary environmental factors that contribute to the development of conduct disorders
  and antisocial behavior are:_____
  _____

    C. A Complex Pathway of Risks

- Most behavior problems are the accumulated effect of exposure to_____
  _____

V. Identification and Assessment

    A. Screening Tests

- Behavior Rating Profile (BRP–2)

- Child Behavior Checklist (CBCL)

- Systematic Screening for Behavioral Disorders (SSBD)

- Behavioral and Emotional Rating Scale (BERS)

    B. Projective Tests

- Consist of ambiguous stimuli (e.g., Rorschach Test) or open-ended tasks. It is assumed that
  responses to items that have no right or wrong answer will_____
  _____

    C. Direct Observation and Measurement of Behavior.

- Behavior can be measured objectively along several dimensions:_____
  _____

D. Functional Behavioral Assessment

- FBA is a systematic process of gathering information to help IEP teams understand why a student is _____

- The information is then used to guide the development of _____

- Functional analysis is the systematic manipulation of several antecedent or consequent events surrounding the target behavior in an attempt to _____

VI. Educational Approaches

A. Curriculum Goals

- Social Skills

- Academic Skills

B. Behavior Management

- Discipline and Schoolwide Systems of Behavior Support

- Classroom Management

- Self-Management

- Peer Mediation and Support

C. Fostering Strong Teacher-Student Relationships

- Differential acceptance means _____
_____

- Having an empathetic relationship with a child refers to a teacher's ability_____
_____
_____

VII. A Focus on Alterable Variables

- Bloom (1980) uses the term *alterable variables* to refer_____
_____

VIII. Educational Placement Alternatives

- Slightly more than half of all students with EBD receive their education in separate classrooms, special schools, and residential facilities.

- Most students receiving special education because of emotional or behavioral disorders have serious, long-standing problems that require _____

_____

IX. Current Issues and Future Trends

    A. Serving All Students with Emotional and Behavioral Disorders

    B. Preventing Emotional and Behavioral Disorders

    C. Disciplining Students with Disabilities

    D. Improving Services for Youth in the Juvenile Corrections Systems

    E. Developing Wraparound Systems of Comprehensive Care

    F. Challenges, Achievements, and Advocacy

Homework

Write a 2- to 3-page paper on one of the following topics.

1. About 43% of the children receiving specialized services for emotional and behavioral disorders have a diagnosis of ADHD. Research indicates that stimulant medication is effective for treating ADHD-related symptoms (impulsivity, hyperactivity, and inattention). However, the data on the effects of medication on social and academic skills are less clear. A recent article by Forness, Kavale, Crenshaw, and Sweeny (2000), leading authorities on behavior disorders, claimed that *not* using stimulants to treat ADHD verges on educational malpractice. Should stimulant medication be a treatment of choice for students with ADHD? What responsibilities does the teacher have in the process of determining treatment options? What responsibilities does the teacher have in ensuring that stimulant medication is an effective treatment in terms of both social and academic performance?

2. It has been suggested that one reason schools do not use systematic screening and identification methods for suspected emotional and behavioral disorders is that many more children would be identified and that this would create a financial burden to the school. Do you think that this is a valid claim? Would you feel the same if you were a member of the school board? If you were the principal?

CD-ROM Questions

1. Compare and contrast the response cards and the response system strategy. What are the advantages and disadvantages of each approach?

   School: Dunkirk Middle School
   Videos and Commentaries: Response Cards & Response System

2. Describe how a student included in a general education class can benefit from the response cards and numbered-heads-together strategies?

   School: Dunkirk Elementary School
   Videos and Commentaries: Response Cards & Numbered Heads

3. Describe a proactive and positive classroom management strategy similar to "beans in a jar" that you could implement in an upper-grade elementary classroom.

   School: Como Elementary School
   Videos and Commentaries: Classroom Management & Class Reward

4. Describe a technique you could use to catch students being good.

   School: Oakstone Academy
   Videos and Commentaries: Teacher Praise

5. How does a teacher know when her praise is effective?

   School: Oakstone Academy
   Videos and Commentaries: Teacher Praise

Self-Check Quiz _____

True/False

1. A child who is socially maladjusted is, by IDEA standards, emotionally disordered.

2. The single best predictor of delinquency in adolescence is a pattern of antisocial behavior as a preschooler.

3. It is not necessary to understand the etiology (cause) of a student's emotional or behavioral disorder in order to effectively serve that student.

4. Compared to other disabilities, children with emotional and behavioral disorders tend to be served in less restrictive settings.

5. A child who exhibits superior academic achievement can be identified as emotionally disordered, given IDEA and CCBD definitions.

6. The use of response cards increases active participation for emotionally disordered students.

7. The purpose of screening is to identify children who qualify for special education services.

8. The number of children served under IDEA for emotional disturbance indicates that an underidentification of these children is occurring.

9. Girls are less likely than boys to be identified for special education for emotional or behavioral disorders because physical differences make them less of a visible threat to school personnel.

10. Data on juvenile delinquents indicate that only about 60% of criminal acts by juveniles are reported, making the extent of juvenile crime unknown.

11. Biological factors, particularly temperament, are a likely cause of most emotional and behavioral disorders.

12. Children with internalizing disorders are more likely to be underidentified than those with externalizing disorders.

13. Observations are too subjective to be a useful part of assessment.

14. The most important aspect in an effective classroom management program is that the teacher react immediately and consistently to inappropriate behaviors.

15. Fewer than 20% of students with emotional or behavioral disorders receive services in special schools or residential placements.

Essay Questions

1. For a fictitious student with a behavioral disorder, write a history in which you illustrate three factors that may have contributed to the formation of his disability.

2. What components do most definitions of emotional and behavioral disorders have in common?

CHAPTER SEVEN
AUTISM SPECTRUM DISORDERS

Focus Questions _____

- **How might instruction be designed so that some of the behaviors characteristic of autism spectrum disorders become strengths for the child as a learner?**

Although children diagnosed with ASD share a number of common behavioral characteristics, it is important to recognize they are often more different than alike. It is therefore imperative for a teacher to determine what the child is good at doing. For example, some children with ASD may not respond well to verbal directions but are very good at following written directions. For those children it is probably best to give written directions. Other children may be very good at following a set routine but have trouble when the routine is changed. For those children it may be better to start each school day with a set routine and slowly make changes as the school year continues. Some students with ASD develop intense interests in particular toys or activities. A teacher can use these interests to motivate the student to learn important social skills. These are just three examples of the myriad ways in which a teacher may make accommodations based on a child's strengths.

- **What factors might account for the sharp rise in the prevalence of autism spectrum disorders in recent years?**

Probably the biggest single factor that has contributed to the rise in the prevalence of ASD is improvements in assessment procedures that can diagnose the disorder at an earlier age. Before these improvements a child with ASD may have been misdiagnosed or diagnosed later in life. Because of the improvements in assessment and screening, the public has become more aware of the disorder. A third factor that may contribute to the rising prevalence is the improvement and greater availability of educational services, particularly applied behavior analysis.

- **Why is early and intensive intervention especially critical for children with autism?**

Like most potentially debilitating conditions, the earlier the condition is diagnosed, the earlier treatment can begin, and often the prognosis for a more typical life is improved. This appears to be critical for children diagnosed with ASD. Early, intensive, behavior-analytic-based instruction has been scientifically demonstrated to improve communication, language, and social skills to such an extent that some children with ASD have been able to succeed in general education classrooms.

- **What skills are most important for a teacher of students with autism spectrum disorders?**

Teaching children with ASD requires a teacher to be well organized, task oriented, attuned to small but cumulative improvements in skill acquisition, and well versed in effective teaching strategies. However, the same can be said about teaching any child. Nevertheless, because children diagnosed with ASD can be among the most difficult to teach, these skills are particularly important for teachers of children with ASD.

- **Why are fads and unproven interventions so prevalent in the treatment of children with autism?**

It has been said that education proceeds from revolution rather than evolution. What that means is that unproven fads have been a part of education for a very long time. Unfortunately, this is especially true for the treatment of ASD. Because the causes of ASD are poorly understood, seemingly plausible theories for treatment are presented in the absence of proof. If these theories are presented by credible authority figures and supplemented with testimonials, parents and educators are likely to give the unproven treatment credence. Because of the characteristics and severity of the disorder, hope and hype often replace reason and evidence when determining what is and what is not an effective treatment. The best way teachers can protect themselves from fad treatments is to ask for the data on the treatment's effectiveness for children like the ones they teach, and evaluate the believability independently from those promoting the treatment.

Essential Concepts _____

- Autism is the name given to any of five related childhood neurobehavioral syndromes subsumed under the term *pervasive developmental disorder (PDD)*. Most professionals now use the term *autism spectrum disorder (ASD)*. The five subtypes are autistic disorder, Asperger syndrome, Rett's syndrome, childhood disintegrative disorder, and pervasive developmental disorder—not otherwise specified. The disorders are differentiated from one another primarily by age of onset and severity of the symptoms. ASD is commonly diagnosed through the use of various assessments of overt behavior.

- ASD is characterized by impaired social skills, language impairments, deficits in intellectual functioning, ritualistic and repetitive behavior patterns, and uneven development of skill acquisition. Although popularly portrayed in many movies (i.e., *Rain Man*) autistic savants are very rare.

- Various theories as to causes of the disorder have been proposed through the years, yet the exact cause of the disorder is not known. It was once thought that uncaring parents were to blame. More recently, it has been proposed that routine childhood immunizations could be the reason. However, both theories have not survived in light of scientific evidence. Experts now suspect that both biological and environmental factors may be responsible for causing the disorder.

- Students with ASD constitute the fastest growing category in special education and are among the most difficult students to teach. Nevertheless, research has shown that carefully planned and delivered instruction together with frequent measurement of progress can improve the skills of children with ASD. Even more encouraging are the results of intensive, behavior-analytic-based, early intervention for the long-term prognosis of children with ASD.

- Because of the characteristics and severity of the disorder, the treatment of ASD has been fraught with unproven treatments and exaggerated claims of treatment effectiveness. Fortunately, there is a growing body of scientifically proven teaching strategies and tactics that are becoming more accessible to parents and teachers.

Objectives _____

DEFINITIONS
1. List the five subtypes of ASD according to the DSM-IV.
2. List the two components of the educational definition in IDEA.

CHARACTERISTICS
1. Describe the academic and social skills deficits associated with ASD.

SCREENING AND DIAGNOSIS
1. List the most commonly used screening devices for ASD.
2. Describe how a child might be given the diagnosis of ASD.

PREVALENCE
1. List the prevalence estimates for children with ASD.
2. Describe the possible reasons why there has been a marked increase in the prevalence of the disorder.

CAUSES
1. List the hypothesized causes of ASD.
2. List the three reasons why educators should not place too much emphasis on theories linking ASD with uncaring parents or to routine immunizations.

EDUCATIONAL APPROACHES
1. Discuss the importance of early intensive behavioral intervention.
2. Describe the important historical events in the education of children with ASD.
3. Define applied behavior analysis.
4. Describe the teaching strategies based on ABA.
5. Describe the teaching strategies to help children with ASD learn to increase their independence in the classroom.

EDUCATIONAL PLACEMENT ALTERNATIVES
1. Identify and describe the various placement alternatives for students with ASD.

CURRENT ISSUES AND FUTURE TRENDS
1. Describe the possible reasons behind the use of "fad" educational treatments for children with ASD.
2. Describe why facilitated communication and secretin have been shown to be unproven treatments.

Chapter Seven at a Glance

Main Topics	Key Points	Key Terms
Autism Spectrum Disorders		
Definitions	The DSM-IV definitions are as follows:	Pervasive developmental disorders
	Autistic disorder: onset before age 3, impairment of social interaction and communication, and stereotypy	Autistic disorder
		Asperger syndrome
	Asperger syndrome: mild end of autism spectrum	Rhett's syndrome
		Childhood disintegrative disorder
	Rhett's syndrome: distinct neurological condition followed by an apparently normal infancy	PDD-NOS
	Childhood disintegrative disorder: age of onset after age 2	
	Pervasive developmental disorder: autistic behavior, significantly impaired socialization.	
	IDEA defines autism spectrum disorders as a developmental disability affecting communication and social interaction. It is evident before age 3 and adversely affects a child's performance.	
Characteristics	The characteristics of children with autism include: impaired social relationships, communication and language deficits, varying levels of intellectual functioning, uneven skill development, unusual responsiveness to sensory stimuli, insistence on sameness and perseveration, ritualistic and unusual behavior patterns	Echolalia
		Autistic savants
		Overselectivity
		Stereotypic behavior
Screening and Diagnosis	Autism can be reliably diagnosed at 18 months of age.	
	Screening of babies showing early warning signs is critical because early diagnosis is correlated with dramatically better outcomes.	
	Diagnoses are made according to the criteria of the DSM-IV.	
Prevalence	Autism is the fastest growing category in special education. Not long ago, autism was considered a rare disorder, with an estimated incidence of about 6.5 in 10,000 children. More recent estimates are 20 in 10,000 children.	
	In the 2003–2004 school year, 140,473 students ages 6 to 21 received special education services under the category of autism.	

Chapter Seven at a Glance

Main Topics	Key Points	Key Terms
Causes	For a long time it was thought that parents who were indifferent to the emotional needs of their children caused autism. No causal link between parental personality and autism has ever been discovered.	
	Recent research shows a clear biological origin of autism in the form of abnormal brain development, structure, and/or neurobiochemistry. Numerous genetic links to autism have been established, but we still do not completely understand their causal relationships.	
	It is not known what causes autism, although research continues to get us closer to answering that question.	
	There is no evidence of childhood vaccinations causing autism	
Educational Approaches	Children with autism require carefully planned, meticulously delivered, and continually evaluated and analyzed instruction. Early intensive behavioral intervention is critical.	Applied behavior analysis Discrete trial training (DTT)
	As a treatment, applied behavior analysis shows great evidence of its effectiveness.	
	Strategies, such as social stories and picture activity schedules, help children with autism cope with social situations and increase their independence in the classroom.	
Educational Placement Alternatives	During the 2003–2004 school year, approximately 27% of students with autism were educated in the regular classroom, with 18% being served in resource room programs and 44% in separate classes. About 11% of students with autism attended special schools or residential facilities.	
	It is important to realize that the regular classroom will not be the least restrictive environment for all children with autism spectrum disorders.	
	Instruction in the resource room typically features a high frequency of instructional trials per minute, strategies for promoting generalization of newly learned skills, and continuous assessment for making timely instructional decisions.	
Current Issues and Future Trends	A serious problem in the field of autism is the popularity of unproven educational interventions and therapies.	
	Parents and professionals should select autism treatments after careful and systematic evaluations of scientific evidence of their effects and benefits.	

Guided Review

I. Definitions

    A. Definitions of Autism Spectrum Disorders in DSM-IV

- Autistic disorder: _____

    _____

- Asperger syndrome: _____

    _____

- Rhett's syndrome: _____

    _____

- Childhood disintegrative disorder: _____

    _____

- Pervasive developmental disorder: _____

    _____

    B. Educational Definition of Autism in IDEA

- Developmental disability affecting communication and social interaction: _____

    _____

II. Characteristics

- Impaired social _____

- Communication and _____

- Varying levels of intellectual functioning, uneven skill development

- Unusual responsiveness of _____

- Insistence on sameness and _____

- Ritualistic and _____

- Problem behavior _____

- Positive attributes _____

III. Screening and Diagnosis

    A. Screening

- Early diagnosis is highly correlated _____

- Autism can be reliably diagnosed at _____

- Checklist for Autism in Toddlers (CHAT)

- Modified Checklist for Autism in Toddlers (M-CHAT)

    B. Diagnosis

- Childhood Autism Rating Scale (CARS)

- Autism Diagnostic Interview—Revised

- Gilliam Autism Rating Scale (GARS)

- Asperger Syndrome Diagnostic Scale (ASDS)

IV. Prevalence

- Fastest growing _____

- In the 2003–2004 school year, _____ students ages 6 to 21 received special education services under the category of autism

V. Causes

- The cause of autism is unknown

- There is a clear biological origin of autism in the form of _____

    _____

- Numerous _____ links to autism have been established

- No evidence of childhood vaccinations causing autism

VI. Educational Approaches

    A. Critical Importance of Early Intensive Behavioral Intervention_____

    _____

    B. Applied Behavior Analysis

- Strategies for shifting student's response to _____

- Alternative forms of _____

- _____ interventions

- Errorless discrimination learning

- Generalization

- _____ of challenging behavior

- Pivotal response intervention

- Naturalistic language strategies

C. Strategies to Help Children with Autism Cope with Social Situations and Increase Their Independence in the Classroom

- Social stories _____

  _____

- Picture activity schedules _____

  _____

VII. Educational Placement Alternatives

A. Regular Classroom

B. Resource Room

VIII. Current Issues and Future Trends

- Although some children with autism have progressed so significantly that they no longer carry the diagnostic label, the opinions of experts differ greatly on the issue of_____

- A serious problem in the field of autism is the popularity of_____

  _____

- Parents and professionals should select autism treatments on the basis of careful and systematic evaluations _____

Homework

Write a 2- to 3-page paper on the following topic.

Throughout the country, many parents of children with autism have begun suing school districts for extramural educational services supplied by behavior analysts. What role should parents have in determining curriculum and instruction for their children? Should school districts have to pay for these services?

CD-ROM Questions

1. What are characteristics of intensive, specialized, and focused instruction for children with autism?

    School: Millennium Community School
    Videos and Commentaries: All

2. Describe a playground or recess activity that a teacher could use to increase the social interactions of a child with autism and his or her same-age peers.

    School: Millennium Community School
    Videos and Commentaries: Social Skills

Self-Check Quiz

True/False

1. Facilitated communication and secretin therapy have validated scientific support for the treatment of autism.

2. Having autism often precludes meaningful achievements.

3. Autism is one of five disorders of early childhood subsumed under the umbrella term *pervasive development disorder (PDD)*.

4. Most individuals with autism also have intellectual impairments.

5. Lovaas's (1987) study seems to indicate that few children with autism can make significant gains in communication or social skills.

6. Most individuals with autism have an extraordinary ability in areas such as memorization, mathematical calculations, or music ability while functioning at the mental retardation level in all other areas.

7. IDEA specifies very limited circumstances under which a child is not considered educable (e.g., is comatose) and therefore not entitled to an education.

8. Most individuals with autism appear to have normal development during their first year of life.

9. Students with autism spectrum disorders constitute the fastest-growing category in special education.

10. Applied behavior analysis always involves the use of the discrete trial method.

11. With early, appropriate intervention, the prognosis for autism is good.

12. Teachers of students with autism must prioritize instructional targets for skill deficits rather than target all at once.

13. Girls are as likely as boys to be affected by autism.

14. "Naturalistic teaching" refers to teachers systematically providing feedback to students when they spontaneously demonstrate a skill.

15. Recent research shows a clear biological origin for autism in the form of abnormal brain development, brain structure, and/or neurochemistry.

Essay Questions

1. Describe the general characteristics of autism, including those characteristics associated with the disorder but not necessarily present.

2. Summarize the features of applied behavior analysis.

CHAPTER EIGHT
COMMUNICATION DISORDERS

Focus Questions

- **How are speech and language interrelated?**

Language is a formalized code used by a group of people to communicate with one another. Each language has rules of phonology, morphology, syntax, semantics, and pragmatics that describe how users put sounds and ideas together to convey meaning. Speech is the oral production of language. It is the fastest and most efficient method of communication by language, and it is also one of the most complex and difficult human endeavors.

- **How should a teacher respond to a child who says, "The dogs runned home"? To a child who says, "That foop is dood"?**

Children's words and sentences often differ from adult forms while children are learning language. As their language develops, children will gradually replace incorrect word pronunciations and sentence structures with acceptable adult forms of language. Whether or not the child's language errors are age-appropriate, it is important that the teacher respond to the child's message first before attempting to correct the errors. The teacher can respond to the child's message while modeling correct forms by saying something like, "Really? The dogs ran in the house?" or "I'm glad you think that food is good." There are a variety of approaches for treating speech and language problems, but speech-language pathologists are increasingly employing naturalistic interventions to help children develop and use language skills.

- **What are common elements of effective interventions for speech and language impairments?**

A wide variety of approaches have been used successfully to treat speech and language impairments. No matter what the approach to treatment, children with language disorders need to be around children and adults with something interesting to talk about. Language is an interactive, interpersonal process, and naturally occurring intervention formats should be used to expose children with language disorders to a wide range of stimuli, experiences, contexts, and people. Effective speech-language pathologists establish specific goals and objectives, keep precise records of their students' performance, and arrange the learning environment so that each child's efforts at communication will be rewarded and enjoyable.

- **What are the most important functions of augmentative and alternative communication?**

Augmentative and alternative communication (AAC) refers to a diverse set of strategies and methods to assist individuals who are unable to meet their communication needs through speech or writing. The three components of AAC are a representational symbol set, a means for selecting symbols, and a means for transmitting symbols.

- **Why are naturalistic interventions more likely to result in maintenance and generalization of a child's new speech and language skills?**

Naturalistic interventions occur in real or simulated activities that naturally occur in the home, school, or community environments in which a child normally functions. Naturalistic interventions (also known as *milieu teaching strategies*) are characterized by their use of dispersed learning trials, attempts to base teaching on the child's attention, leading with the context of normal conversational interchanges, and orientation toward teaching the form and content of language in the context of normal use. Naturalistic approaches are more likely to promote generalization of language skills because instruction occurs in the context of the child's normal daily interactions. This eliminates the step of having to carry over skills learned in didactic, contrived situations to natural situations.

Essential Concepts

- Communication is necessary in nearly every aspect of a child's day-to-day routine; its role in learning social and academic skills is critical. Disorders involving student's articulation, voice quality, fluency, or use and understanding of language can significantly influence the student's learning. It is no wonder that speech and language disorders represents the second largest disability category in terms of the number of children served.

- Normal language development follows a relatively predictable sequence. Most children learn to use language without direct instruction by age 5. When a child's language development deviates from the norm to such an extent that he or she has serious difficulties in learning and in interpersonal relations, the child is said to have a communication disorder. Special education is needed when a communication disorder adversely affects educational performance.

- As many as 5% of school-age children have speech impairments serious enough to warrant attention. Nearly twice as many boys as girls have speech impairments. Children with articulation problems represent the largest category of speech-language impairments.

- Communication disorders that are organic are attributed to a specific physical cause. Most communication disorders, however, do not have a known physical origin. Environmental influences, such as the child's opportunity to learn speech and language, are thought to be the major causes of many communication disorders.

- There are various treatment approaches to speech and language disorders. With few exceptions, however, treatment of children with such disorders involves aspects of their environment where they need to communicate. The goal of most treatment programs is to teach children to communicate with a variety of other individuals and across a variety of circumstances.

- Augmentative and alternative communication (AAC) may be necessary in severe situations. An augmentative communication system is designed to supplement and enhance a person's communication capabilities.

Objectives

DEFINITIONS
1. List the 3 elements that are needed for communication to occur.
2. Describe the 4 functions of language
3. Define *language*.
4. List and provide examples of the 5 dimensions of language.
5. Define *speech*.
6. Define *communication disorder*.
7. Compare and contrast the definitions of speech impairments and language disorders.

CHARACTERISTICS
1. Identify and describe the types of communication disorders.

PREVALENCE
1. List the percentage data for students receiving special education services for speech or language impairments.

CAUSES
1. Identify the probable causes of some speech and language disorders.

IDENTIFICATION AND ASSESSMENT
1. Describe the evaluation components for speech and language disorders.

EDUCATIONAL APPROACHES
1. Describe the treatment options for articulation, phonological, and fluency problems.
2. Define and provide examples of augmentative and alternative communication.

EDUCATIONAL PLACEMENT ALTERNATIVES
1. Describe the continuum of educational placements for students with communication disorders

CURRENT ISSUES AND FUTURE TRENDS
1. Discuss the controversy regarding the use of speech and language pathologists in the classroom.

Chapter Eight at a Glance

Main Topics	Key Points	Key Terms
Communication Disorders		paralinguistic codes nonlinguistic cues phonology morphology syntax semantics pragmatics phonation resonance articulation
Definitions	Communication involves encoding, transmitting, and decoding messages.	
	Language is a formalized code used by a group of people to communicate with one another.	
	The five dimensions of language are phonology, morphology, syntax, semantics, and pragmatics.	
	Knowledge of normal language development can help the special educator determine whether a particular child is simply developing language at a slower-than-normal rate or whether the child shows an abnormal pattern of language development.	expressive language disorder receptive language disorder dialects
	Most children follow a relatively predictable sequence in their acquisition of speech and language.	
	ASHA defines a communication disorder as an impairment in the ability to receive, send, process, and comprehend concepts of verbal, nonverbal, and graphic symbols systems.	
	Speech is impaired when it deviates so far from the speech of other people that it calls attention to itself, interferes with communication, or provokes distress in the speaker or listener. Three basic types of speech impairments are articulation disorders, fluency disorders, and voice disorders.	
	It is always important to keep the speaker's age, education, and cultural background in mind when determining whether speech is impaired.	
	The way each of us speaks is the result of a complex mix of influences including race and ethnicity, socioeconomic class, education, occupation, geographical region, and peer group identification. Every language contains a variety of forms called dialects.	
Characteristics	The four basic kinds of sound speech errors are distortions, substitutions, omissions, and additions.	distortions substitutions omissions additions fluency disorders cluttering dysphonia hypernasality hyponasality
	A severe articulation disorder is present when a child pronounces many sounds so poorly that her speech is unintelligible most of the time.	
	Children with phonological disorders are especially at risk in spelling and reading.	
	Dysphonia describes any condition of poor or unpleasant voice quality.	

Chapter Eight at a Glance

Main Topics	Key Points	Key Terms
Prevalence	A little more than 2% of school-age children receive special education for speech and language impairments, the second largest disability category under IDEA.	
	Children with articulation and spoken language problems represent the largest category of speech-language impairments.	
Causes	Most communication disorders are not considered organic but are classified as functional.	functional communication cleft palate dysarthria aphasia
	Factors that contribute to language disorders include cognitive limitations or mental retardation, hearing impairments, behavioral disorders, and environmental deprivation.	
Identification and Assessment	Evaluation components include case history and physical examination, articulation test, hearing test, auditory discrimination test, phonological awareness and processing, vocabulary and language development, language samples, and observation in natural settings.	
Educational Approaches	The speech-language pathologist is the school-based professional with the primary responsibility for identifying, evaluating, and providing therapeutic services.	naturalistic interventions mileu teaching strategies AAC symbol systems
	Methods for treating speech and language disorders include discrimination and production activities, principles and self-monitoring, direct vocal rehabilitation, exploration of expressive language, and naturalistic interventions.	
	Augmentative and alternative communication (AAC) has three components: a representational symbol set, a means for selecting symbols, and a means for transmitting symbols.	
Educational Placement Alternatives	Eighty-nine percent of children with speech and language impairments are served in regular classrooms, 6.5% in resource rooms, and 4.5% in separate classes.	
	The following service delivery models are used within these three placements: monitoring, pull-out, collaborative consultation, classroom-based, self-contained classroom, and community-based.	
Current Issues and Future Trends	Speech-language professionals will deal with the controversy as to whether services should take a therapeutic versus educational focus.	
	Across the day interventions mean that interventions must be applicable not only in the classroom but by teachers and parents.	

Guided Review

I. Definitions

    A. Communication involves encoding, transmitting, and _____

        • Communication has the following important functions between teachers and children: _____

        _____

    B. Language

        • The five dimensions of language are_____

        _____

    C. Speech

        • Speech is the _____

        • Speech sounds are the product of the following four separate but related processes:_____

        _____

    D. Normal Development of Speech and Language

    E. Communication Disorders Defined

        • ASHA defines a communication disorder as an impairment in the ability to receive, send,

        process, and comprehend concepts of_____

        • Speech is impaired when it deviates so far from the speech of other people that it _____

        _____

        • It is always important to keep the speaker's _____ in
        mind when determining whether speech is impaired.

        • Language disorders may involve the_____

        • Children who have difficulty understanding language have a(n) _____ language
        disorder.

        • Children who have difficulty producing language have a(n) _____ language
        disorder.

    F. Communication Differences Are Not Disorders

        • The way each of us speaks is the result of a complex mix of influences including _____

        _____

        _____

II. Characteristics

    A. Speech Sound Errors

- The four basic kinds of speech sound errors are _____

- A severe articulation disorder is present when _____

- Children with phonological disorders are apt to experience problems in _____

        _____

    B. Fluency Disorders

- Stuttering and cluttering are examples of fluency disorders.

    C. Voice Disorders

- Dysphonia describes any condition of_____

- A phonation disorder causes the voice to sound _____ most of the time.

- Resonance disorders are _____ and _____

    D. Language Impairments

- An expressive language impairment interferes with _____ of language

- A receptive language impairment interferes with _____ of language

III. Prevalence

- A little more than 2% of school-age children receive special education for speech and language impairments, the second largest disability category under IDEA

- Approximately 50% of children who receive special education services for _____ also have communication disorders

- Nearly twice as many boys as girls have speech impairments

IV. Causes

- Most communication disorders are not considered _____ but are classified as _____

- A functional communication disorder cannot be ascribed to a specific physical condition, and its origin is not completely known

- Physical causes of speech impairments include _____

- Factors that contribute to language disorders include _____

_____

- Aphasia describes a loss of the ability to _____

V. Identification and Assessment

- Evaluation components include _____

_____

_____

VI. Educational Approaches

- The speech-language pathologist is the school-based professional with the primary responsibility

  for _____

  _____

  A. Treating Speech Sound Errors

  - Articulation errors _____

  - Phonological errors _____

  B. Treating Fluency Disorders

  - No single method has been recognized as most effective

  C. Treating Voice Disorders

  D. Treating Language Disorders

  - Speech language pathologists are increasingly employing _____

  E. Augmentative and Alternative Communication

  - AAC has three components: _____

  _____

VII. Educational Placement Alternatives

- Placement options for students with speech and language impairments are _____

  _____

VIII. Current Issues and Future Trends

- Specialists will probably function even more _____ in the future.

- Speech and language professionals will deal with the controversy as to whether services should

  take a _____ versus _____ focus

- Changing populations means growing _____ and more children

  with _____ being served.

Homework _____

Write a 2- to 3-page paper on one of the following topics.

1. Should all children in the United States be expected to speak Standard American English regardless of their cultural, social, or geographic background? Explain why or why not.

2. A speech and language pathologist (SLP) has been traditionally responsible for providing services to students with communication disorders, usually with pull-out sessions. With the enhanced emphasis on inclusion, their role appears to be changing. In the Current Issues and Future Trends section, Heward discusses a few of the issues related to SLP. However, SLPs are not trained teachers and hold no certification in teaching. In your paper, address the following questions: What role should an SLP take in the classroom? Should SLPs also be trained in instructional methods? How can a teacher help integrate the SLP in the classroom? See the Companion Website for links to assist you in developing your answer.

Self-Check Quiz _____

True/False

1. The term *language learning disabilities* is used to refer to receptive and/or expressive language disorders.

2. Communication disorders represent the second largest category in special education.

3. Voice disorders involve two basic types: phonation and resonance.

4. To be eligible for special education services, a child's communication disorder must have an adverse effect on learning.

5. The most effective format for language intervention is to eliminate distracting stimuli by working in a one-to-one setting.

6. Paralinguistic codes are speech modifications (e.g., intonation, pauses) that change form and meaning of a message.

7. To identify children who may need speech-language screening requires certified speech-language pathologists because of the complexity of these disorders.

8. *Articulation disorders* and *phonological disorders* are equivalent terms to describe problems with speech.

9. The letter "s" at the end of the word "shoes" is a morpheme because it carries meaning.

10. Most normally developing children need some form of drilling or direct instruction to move from developmental forms to acceptable adult forms of speech and language.

11. Most communication involves nonspeech methods.

12. An adult who suffers a stroke that causes her to lose the ability to use language has aphasia.

13. Almost half of those who receive special education because of another primary disability also have a communication disorder.

14. Most languages have a logical and natural structure between a set of sounds and what they represent.

15. A person with good semantics is one who understands relationships between words such as synonyms, and knows that context changes word meanings.

Essay Questions

1. Describe the characteristics, basics of treatment by clinician and teacher, and prognosis for stuttering.

2. Explain the concept of *dialect* and its relationship to communication disorders.

CHAPTER NINE
DEAFNESS AND HEARING LOSS

Focus Questions

- **In what ways do the child who is deaf and the child who is hard of hearing differ?**

Children who are deaf may be able to perceive some sound but are unable to use their hearing to understand speech. Deaf children develop speech and language skills mainly through their sense of sight. Children who are hard of hearing, on the other hand, have a significant hearing loss that makes special adaptations necessary. It is possible, however, for these children to respond to speech and other auditory stimuli. Children who are hard of hearing develop their speech and language skills mainly through the sense of hearing.

- **How do students who identify culturally with the Deaf community view hearing impairment?**

As discussed earlier in the text, a disability may be a handicap in one environment but not in another. There may be no condition for which this is more true than a hearing impairment. When answering this question, it may be helpful to consider another question, "Is it 'nature' that attaches enormous importance to hearing in human development and learning, or is it society?" Most people live in a world where hearing is vital to virtually every aspect of their lives. Yet there exists a "Deaf culture" that insists it is not a disability to be hearing impaired.

- **Why can't reading simply replace speech as a means of learning and understanding English?**

Years before children learn through reading, hearing is used to acquire information and develop expressive and receptive language skills. By the time typically hearing children enter school, they have a vocabulary of over 5,000 words and have already had 100 million meaningful contacts with language. Even after children learn to read, a good deal of what they learn is acquired through auditory means. Children who learn only through reading would miss out on many critical opportunities to learn and to develop basic communication skills.

- **How do oral/aural, total communication, and bilingual-bicultural approaches differ in their philosophies and teaching methods?**

The fundamental disagreement concerns the extent to which children who are deaf should express themselves through speech and perceive the communication of others through speechreading and residual hearing. Educators who primarily utilize the oral approach emphasize the development of speech and language and view speech as essential for integration into the hearing world; they often discourage the use of sign language and other gestures. Educators who utilize a total communication approach (i.e., use of sign language, gestures, cues, fingerspelling, and other manual means used along with speech) believe this to be a more natural way of communicating, and believe that this approach enables children who are hearing impaired to more fully express themselves and understand the communication of others.

- **Why has American Sign Language (ASL) not been fully accepted as the language of instruction in educational programs for deaf children?**

American Sign Language (ASL) is structured to accommodate individuals who are hearing impaired, not individuals with hearing. Because ASL has its own vocabulary, syntax, and grammatical rules, it does not correspond exactly to spoken or written English. This makes precise word-for-word translations between ASL and English just as difficult as word-for-word translations between different spoken languages. Many educators fail to see that ASL is a language in its own right, not a manual communication of English.

Essential Concepts _____

- Hearing impairments are usually viewed as one of the more significant disabilities, perhaps because so much of our learning comes to us through the sense of hearing. Yet many people with hearing impairments and many who are deaf view hearing loss not as a disability but as a linguistic difference. In addition, most people who are hearing impaired have typical cognitive abilities and can and often do vociferously advocate for their own rights.

- As with other disabilities, there is no absolute determination of what constitutes impaired hearing. Although children who are deaf are not able to use their hearing to understand speech, they may perceive some sounds. Children who are hard of hearing also have a significant hearing loss, but unlike deaf children, they can respond to speech and other auditory stimuli.

- For many years educators have debated the most appropriate instructional methods for these children. Educational programs with an oral emphasis view speech as essential for integration into the hearing world. Much attention is given to amplification, auditory training, speechreading, and the use of technological aids. Other educators utilize a total communication approach with students with impaired hearing. This approach uses a variety of methods to assist the child in expressing, receiving, and developing language. Still others believe that deafness merely reflects a linguistic difference, not a disability; therefore, they advocate for the exclusive use of ASL as the method of instruction.

- Many children with hearing impairments lag far behind their hearing peers in academic achievement, and the achievement gap usually widens as they get older. This suggests that more effort needs to be made in enhancing the curriculum and instructions for students with hearing impairments.

- The debate over communication and instructional methods for students with impaired hearing is likely to continue because research has yet to provide a definitive answer to the question of which communication method is best. Fortunately, technological advances are improving the communication abilities of many individuals with hearing impairments, and future technological advances may enable educators to analyze and track their language development with much greater precision. This information could be used to design more appropriate language instruction.

Objectives _____

DEFINITIONS
1. Define *deaf*.
2. Define *hard of hearing*.
3. Describe how humans hear.
4. Discuss why some individuals who are hard of hearing or deaf believe that deafness is a cultural phenomenon and not a disability.

CHARACTERISTICS
1. Identify the three qualifications that need to be made when attempting to describe this population.
2. Describe academic outcomes and the behavioral characteristics of many children with hearing impairments.

PREVALENCE
1. List the prevalence figures for hard of hearing and deafness.

TYPES AND CAUSES OF HEARING LOSS
1. Identify the two main types of hearing loss.
2. Discuss why degree and age of onset of hearing loss are important.
3. List the causes of hearing loss.

IDENTIFICATION AND ASSESSMENT

1. Describe the process for determining if a person is hard of hearing or deaf.

TECHNOLOGIES AND SUPPORTS

1. List the types of supports that amplify or provide sound.
2. List the types of supports that supplement or replace sound.

EDUCATIONAL APPROACHES

1. Define and describe the oral/aural approach.
2. Define and describe the total communication approach.
3. Define and describe the bilingual-bicultural approach.
4. Compare and contrast the three approaches.

EDUCATIONAL PLACEMENT ALTERNATIVES

1. Describe the continuum of educational placements for students with hearing impairments.

CURRENT ISSUES AND FUTURE TRENDS

1. Discuss the controversy regarding the most appropriate instructional methods for children who are deaf.

Chapter Nine at a Glance

Main Topics	Key Points	Key Terms
Deafness and Hearing Loss Definitions	IDEA defines *hearing impairment* as a hearing loss that adversely affects educational performance. Children who are deaf use vision as their primary modality for learning and communication, while children who are hard of hearing are able to use their hearing to understand speech. Many people who are deaf do not view their hearing loss as a disability and consider the term *hearing impairment* inappropriate and demeaning. The sense of hearing is a complex and not completely understood process. Sound is measured in decibels (intensity) and hertz (frequency).	hearing impairment deaf residual hearing hard of hearing audition auditory canal tympanic membrane ossicles cochlea decibels hertz
Characteristics	Students with hearing loss are a heterogeneous group. A child who is unable to hear the speech sounds of other people will not learn speech and language spontaneously. Atypical speech is common for many children with hearing impairments. The academic problems of students who are deaf are largely attributable to the mismatch between their perceptual abilities and the demands of spoken and written English. The extent to which a child with hearing loss successfully interacts depends largely on others' attitudes and the child's ability to communicate in some mutually accepted way.	
Prevalence	According to ASHA, 95 out of every 1,000 people have a chronic hearing loss. About 25% of students who are deaf or hard of hearing have another disabling condition.	
Types and Causes of Hearing Loss	Conductive hearing loss results from abnormalities of the outer or middle ear, and sensorineural hearing loss refers to damage to the inner ear. Hearing loss can be congenital (present at birth) or acquired (appearing after birth). The child whose hearing loss is prelingual (before language is acquired) has educational needs that are very different from the child whose hearing loss is postlingual (after language is acquired). Congenital hearing loss is caused by genetic factors, maternal rubella, CMV, or prematurity. Acquired hearing loss is caused by otitis media, meningitis, Ménière's disease, and noise exposure.	conductive hearing loss sensorineural hearing loss unilateral bilateral congenital acquired prelingual postlingual

Chapter Nine at a Glance

Main Topics	Key Points	Key Terms
Identification and Assessment	Auditory brain stem response and otoacoustic emission screening are used to assess infants.	audiometer
		audiogram
	Pure tone audiometry is used to assess older children and adults, and speech audiometry tests detection and understanding of speech.	speech audiometry
		speech reception threshold
Technologies and Supports	Hearing aids make sounds louder but not necessarily clearer; however, modern hearing aids can differentially amplify frequencies.	cochlear implants
	Group assistive listening devices can solve problems caused by distance, noise, and reverberation in the classroom by establishing a radio link between the teacher and student with hearing loss.	
	Surgically placed cochlear implants stimulate the auditory nerve directly. Many members of the Deaf community are vehemently opposed to cochlear implants.	
	Supports and technologies that replace sound include: interpreters, speech-to-text translation, television captioning, text telephones, and alerting devices.	
Educational Approaches	Oral/aural approaches, which are difficult and time consuming, focus on developing the ability to speak intelligibly. These approaches include auditory learning, speechreading, and cued speech.	auditory learning
		speechreading
		cued speech
	Total communication, the most widely used method of instruction in schools for the deaf, combines speech and manual communication (manually coded English, fingerspelling).	manually coded English
		fingerspelling
		bilingual/bicultural
	The bilingual/bicultural approach focuses on students mastering their first language (American Sign Language), which will enable them to master reading and writing in their second language (English).	American Sign Language
Educational Placement Alternatives	Parents have the option of choosing between their local public school or residential school placement (82% attend local public schools).	continuum of placement options
	Professional and parent organizations are strongly in favor of maintaining the continuum of placement options.	
	A growing number of postsecondary educational opportunities are available to students with hearing loss.	
Current Issues and Future Trends	The bilingual/bicultural approach will probably continue to be used with children served in special schools or self-contained classrooms.	
	Children with hearing loss should have access to the communication modality best suited for their individual needs.	

Guided Review

I. Definitions

- Hearing impairment indicates a hearing loss that_____

- A child who is deaf uses vision as the _____

- A deaf person may perceive some sounds through _____

- Children who are hard of hearing are able to _____

- Many persons who are deaf do not view hearing loss as a_____

A. How We Hear

- Audition, the sense of hearing, is a complex and not completely understood process.

- The auricle funnels sound waves into the _____

- Variations in sound pressure cause the eardrum to _____

- The vibrations of the bones of the middle ear _____

- The inner ear is the most _____ part of the hearing apparatus.

B. The Nature of Sound

- The intensity or loudness in sound is measured in _____

- The frequency, or pitch, of sound is measured in cycles per second or _____

II. Characteristics

- Students with hearing loss comprise an extremely _____ group

- Levels of functioning are influenced by_____

  _____

- Generalizations about how deaf people are supposed to act and feel must be viewed with

  _____

A. English Literacy

- A child who is unable to hear the language of other people will not _____

  _____

- Students with hearing loss have smaller vocabularies and difficulty with _____

- Many deaf students write sentences that are _____

B. Speaking

- Atypical speech is common in many children who are deaf or hard of hearing.

C. Academic Achievement

- Most children with hearing loss have difficulty with _____

- Deafness itself imposes no limitations on the _____

D. Social Functioning

- The extent to which a child with hearing loss successfully interacts depends largely on _____

III. Prevalence

- According to ASHA, *95* out of every 1,000 people have a chronic hearing loss.

- The large majority of persons with hearing loss are adults.

- The U.S. Public Health Service estimates 83 out of 1,000 children have _____

  hearing loss.

- About 25% of students who are deaf or hard of hearing have _____

IV. Types and Causes of Hearing Loss

A. Types and Age at Onset

- Conductive hearing loss results from _____

- Sensorineural hearing loss refers to_____

- Unilateral hearing loss is present in one ear, and bilateral hearing loss is present in both ears.

- Congenital hearing loss is _____, and acquired hearing loss _____

- Prelingual hearing loss and postlingual hearing loss identify whether a hearing loss occurred

B. Causes of Congenital Hearing Loss

- Genetic Factors

- Maternal Rubella

- Congenital Cytomegalovirus (CMV)

- Prematurity

   C. Causes of Acquired Hearing Loss

- Otitis Media

- Meningitis

- Ménière's Disease

- Noise-Induced Hearing Loss

V. Identification and Assessment

   A. Assessment of Infants

- The two most widely used methods of screening for hearing loss measure physiological reactions to sound.

- Auditory brain stem response:_____

     _____

- Otoacoustic emission screening: _____

   B. Pure-Tone Audiometry

- Used to assess the hearing of _____. The results are

     plotted on a chart called a(n) _____

   C. Speech Audiometry

- Speech audiometry tests a person's_____

     _____

   D. Alternative Audiometric Techniques

- Play audiometry

- Operant conditioning audiometry

- Behavior observation audiometry

VI. Technologies and Supports

   A. Technologies That Amplify or Provide Sound

- Modern hearing aids can differentially amplify selected frequencies and be tailored to each child's individual pattern of hearing loss

- Hearing aids make sounds louder but not _____

- The earlier in life a child can be fitted with an appropriate hearing aid, the _____

_____

- Hearing aids offer minimal benefit in noisy reverberant classrooms. Assistive listening

devices can solve problems of_____

- Cochlear implants _____

B. Supports and Technologies That Supplement or Replace Sound

- Interpreters

- Speech-to-Text Translation

- Television Captioning

- Text Telephones

- Alerting Devices

VII. Educational Approaches

A. Oral/Aural Approaches

- Training in producing and understanding speech is incorporated_____

_____

- Oral emphasis programs typically use several means to develop _____

_____

- The oral approach includes _____

B. Total Communication

- Simultaneous presentation of language by _____

- Total communication has become the most widely used method of instruction in schools for the deaf: manually coded English and fingerspelling

C. American Sign Language (ASL) and the Bilingual-Bicultural Approach

- ASL is the language of the Deaf culture in the United States

- ASL is a legitimate _____ in its own right

- ASL does not correspond to _____

- The goal of the bilingual-bicultural education approach is to help deaf students _____

_____

VIII. Educational Placement Alternatives

- Approximately _____ of children who are deaf or hard of hearing attend local public schools

- While full inclusion in regular classrooms has benefited some deaf students, all of the professional and parent organizations involved with educating students who are deaf have issued position

  statements strongly in favor _____

A. Postsecondary Education

- The percentage of students with hearing loss who attend postsecondary educational programs

  has _____

- About _____ of all students with hearing loss go on to receive higher education.

IX. Current Issues and Future Trends

- Given the large percentage of children with hearing loss who are educated in regular classrooms

  for most of the day, it is likely that_____

  _____

- The _____ will probably be used with a growing percentage of the deaf students served in special schools and self-contained classrooms.

- Many leaders of the deaf community do not view deafness as a disability and oppose efforts _____

  _____

- The keys to improving the future for people who are deaf or hard of hearing are access to the language and communication modality best suited to individual needs and preferences, effective instruction with meaningful curriculum, and self-advocacy.

Homework

Write a 2- to 3-page paper on one of the following topics.

1. After reading the Diversity & Exceptionality feature, "Defiantly Deaf: Deaf People Live, Proudly, in Another Culture, but Not a Lessor One," and the Profiles & Perspectives feature, "Deafness: The Dilemma," explain your perspective on the extent to which deafness is a culture and the extent to which deafness is a disability.

2. Select a particular approach or method of instruction used in deaf education (oral/aural, total communication, ASL). Explore and learn about that method. Write a position paper outlining your perspectives and recommendations concerning the approach or method with respect to this question: How might the language and mode of instruction used to teach students who are deaf (or Deaf) support or impede their acquisition of English literacy skills, academic achievement, social functioning, and/or self-concept?

Self-Check Quiz

True/False

1. Most students with a hearing impairment are educated in the public schools.

2. A person who can hear sounds of a frequency between 500 and 5,000 Hz can hear men's voices more easily than women's.

3. Most students who are deaf or hard of hearing also have another disabling condition, such as learning disabilities.

4. A conductive hearing loss originates in the outer or middle ear.

5. Noise exposure is the leading cause of postlingual hearing loss.

6. The main receptor organ for hearing is the tympanic membrane.

7. For the hearing impaired, the development of language and communication skills is the primary objective of all instructional approaches.

8. Nearly all deaf children have some amount of residual hearing.

9. ASL is a visual-spatial form of English.

10. Children with hearing impairments are more likely than their hearing peers to have social and emotional difficulties.

11. Hearing aids work by amplifying all sounds, to enable better use of residual hearing.

12. The bilingual/bicultural approach prioritizes the learning of ASL over English.

13. Deaf infants do not babble, coo, or smile like hearing infants.

14. IDEA requires that the communication needs of a student who is deaf be considered on the IEP.

Essay Questions

1. Distinguish between the terms *deaf* and *Deaf*.

2. Compare and contrast different forms of audiometry.

CHAPTER TEN
BLINDNESS AND LOW VISION

Focus Questions

- **In what ways does loss of vision affect learning?**

Consider all the events in the environment that are perceived through vision. Hearing, taste, touch, and smell help to add detail to what is seen, but it is vision that plays the critical role in learning to interact with the various features of the environment. Sighted individuals may take for granted all of the information obtained through the eyes and the relative ease with which this visual information is learned. It is not difficult to make a list of the academic skills that children with visual impairment will have difficulty learning because of the absence or distortion of visual information. But learning is not limited to academics. Knowing when a classmate or teacher is disappointed or pleased, eating without embarrassment in the school cafeteria, and interacting appropriately in social situations are also largely dependent on visual information. Special instructional methods and equipment are often necessary for children with visual impairment to help them acquire the academic and social skills necessary for independent and productive living.

- **How does the age at which vision is lost affect the student?**

One factor that influences instructional decisions for children with visual impairment is the point in the child's life when the vision loss occurred. Congenital visual impairment is present at birth. Adventitious visual impairment is acquired at some point during a person's life. A child who is adventitiously blind usually retains some visual memory, and the teacher can take advantage of the images the child recalls when designing teaching programs and instructional activities. Teaching the words *dog* and *blue* will be much easier if the child has seen a dog or things that are blue. Children with a congenital visual impairment, however, have no visual history and will often require education programming that makes use of their nonvisual experiences. Learning what dogs are can be accomplished through the sense of touch, but touching dogs is not the same as seeing dogs. Concepts such as blueness, as simple as they are for most normally sighted children to learn, may be impossible for children with congenital visual impairment to understand. Additionally, the level of emotional support and acceptance will differ for children who are adventitiously blind and those who are congenitally blind. The child who must make a sudden adjustment to the loss of vision will probably require a great deal of emotional support.

- **Normally sighted children enter school with a great deal of knowledge about trees. How can a teacher help a student who is congenitally blind learn about trees?**

Because the visual impairment has been present since birth, the child has a total absence of visual memory. Verbal descriptions of the tree may add something to the child's understanding, but the teaching approach will have to rely primarily on direct, firsthand contact with trees through the child's other senses. This design of the teaching program must allow the child to experience a wide range of tactile, olfactory, auditory, and other sensory stimuli, all of which add to the essence of a tree and help convey that trees are of different sizes, shapes, and types. This teaching approach for the concept of a tree will be similar to the teaching approach for the many other concepts that students with visual impairment must learn.

- **What compensatory skills do students with visual impairments need most?**

A basic goal of special education concerns teaching skills for independent and productive living. Academic skills alone will not accomplish this goal. Learning life skills such as cooking, grooming, managing money, participating in leisure activities, and coping with societal expectations are essential parts of any curriculum for exceptional learners. In addition, children with visual impairment should know how to explain their disability to others and to refrain from behaviors such as rocking and head rolling that draw undue and often negative attention to their disabilities. Because most students with visual impairment are educated in regular school settings, it is easy to focus attention exclusively on academic skills. It is important to recognize, however, that academics are but one part of a curriculum necessary to prepare students with visual impairment for life beyond the classroom.

- **How do the educational goals and instructional methods for children with low vision differ from those of children who are blind?**

  As do children in all other categories of exceptionality, children with visual impairments exhibit a wide range of abilities. Children who are identified as blind generally have little or no useful vision. Children with low vision, on the other hand, often have residual vision so that with various types of ocular aids, such as large print or magnifiers, they can use printed materials in their classrooms and communities. Children with visual impairments have different levels of visual ability, but the goal of instruction is the same for all these children: to teach them skills that will enable them to take their place in society as productive, self-sufficient individuals.

Essential Concepts _____

- The legal definition of blindness is based on a person's ability to see clearly at specified distances as well as the adequacy of a person's peripheral vision. The educational definition focuses on the effects of visual impairment on the child's academic performance.

- Children with visual impairment display a wide range of visual capabilities from blindness—the total absence of useful vision—to low vision, which can be quite useful for learning. All of these students, however, require special educational modifications to assist their progress in regular educational programs.

- The age of onset of a visual impairment is an important consideration in programming. Children who have been blind from birth have no visual history to apply to their current learning needs. Adventitiously blind children, on the other hand, have had some visual experiences, which typically facilitate the teaching of many skills.

- By using braille and a host of manipulative, technological, and optical aids, children with visual impairment can participate in academic programs with their normally sighted peers. Academics cannot, however, be the exclusive focus of educational programs. Gaining social skills, meeting expectations, finding suitable work, exploring sexuality, and other basic life experiences are as important as academics. In addition, specialized training in orientation and mobility is essential to ensuring the independence of students who are blind or have low vision.

Objectives _____

DEFINITIONS
1. List the legal definition of blindness.
2. Define *visual acuity* and describe what is meant by *normal vision*.
3. List the educational definition of visual impairment.
4. Discuss why the age of onset is an important concern for special educators.

CHARACTERISTICS
1. Discuss how vision affects other areas of development.

PREVALENCE
1. List the prevalence figures for children with visual impairments.

TYPES AND CAUSES OF VISUAL IMPAIRMENTS
1. Describe how a person sees.
2. Define and describe the causes of visual impairments.

EDUCATIONAL APPROACHES
1. Discuss the types of technological assistance available to students who are blind.
2. Discuss the types of technological assistance available to students with low vision.
3. Define and describe orientation and mobility training.

EDUCATIONAL PLACEMENT ALTERNATIVES
1. Describe the continuum of educational placements for students with visual impairments.

CURRENT ISSUES AND FUTURE TRENDS
1. Discuss the issues facing the future of the education of students with visual impairments.

Chapter Ten at a Glance

Main Topics	Key Points	Key Terms
Blindness and Low Vision		
Definitions	Legal blindness is defined by having visual acuity of 20/200 or less in the better eye after the best possible correction, and/or a field of vision of less than 20 degrees.	visual acuity field of vision legally blind totally blind functionally blind low vision congenital adventitious
	Educational definitions of *totally blind, functionally blind,* and *low vision* focus on the extent to which students are able to use the visual channel for learning.	
	Age of onset (whether the visual impairment is present at birth or acquired later) is an important factor for determining educational programming and support.	
Characteristics	Children with visual impairments need explicit experience with the environment in order to organize and make connections between experiences. Abstract concepts can be particularly difficult for children who cannot see.	incidental learning stereotypic behavior
	Children with low vision have poorer motor skills than sighted children.	
	Some students with visual impairment experience problems with social adjustment and interaction due to limited common experiences with sighted peers; inability to see and use eye contact, facial expressions, and gestures during conversations; and/or stereotypic behavior.	
	The attitudes and behavior of sighted persons may present unnecessary barriers for social participation of students with low vision.	
Prevalence	Children with visual impairments constitute a very small percentage of the school-age population (fewer than 2 children in 1,000).	
Types and Causes of Visual Impairments	Effective vision requires proper functioning of the optical system, the muscular system, and the nervous system.	cornea lens vitreous humor retina ocular motility optic nerve
	Causes of visual impairment are grouped into three categories: refractive errors (e.g., myopia, hyeropia); structural impairments (e.g., cataracts, glaucoma, nystagmus, strabismus); and cortical visual impairments.	
Educational Approaches	Special adaptations for students who are blind include the use of braille for reading and writing; tactile aids and manipulatives (e.g., Cranmer abacus, Speech-Plus talking calculator, embossed relief maps and diagrams); technological aids for reading print (e.g., Optacon, Kurzweil reading system); and assistive computer technology (e.g., magnifying screen images, speech recognition, and conversion of text files into synthesized speech).	braille MAVIS SAVI Optacon

Chapter Ten at a Glance

Main Topics	Key Points	Key Terms
Educational Approaches (continued)	Functional vision cannot be determined by measures of visual acuity and field of vision. Systematic training can help students use their limited vision more effectively.	functional vision orientation mobility laser beam cane Mowat sensor SonicGuide
	Special adaptations for students with low vision include optical devices (e.g., glasses, contacts, small handheld telescopes, magnifiers); large-print text; and a variety of classroom adaptations such as desk lamps, desks with tilting tops, and off-white writing paper.	
	Training in orientation (knowing your location) and mobility (moving safely from one point to another) is necessary for increasing independent functioning for people with visual impairments.	
	Orientation and mobility aids include the long cane, guide dogs, sighted guides, and electronic travel aids.	
	Children with low vision do not develop important listening skills automatically. They need specific instruction in becoming aware of sounds, discriminating differences between sounds, identifying the sources of sounds, and attaching meaning to sounds.	
	Curriculum goals for students with visual impairments should include functional living skills (e.g., cooking, shopping, transportation).	
Educational Placement Alternatives	About 90% of students with visual impairments attend local public schools.	
	In many districts, a specially trained itinerant vision specialist provides support to students with low vision and their regular classroom teachers.	
	The current population of residential schools consists largely of children with visual impairments with additional disabilities, such as mental retardation, hearing impairment, behavioral disorders, and cerebral palsy.	
	Most parents can choose between public day and residential schools for their children with visual impairments.	
Current Issues and Future Trends	Children with visual impairments are likely to receive special education services in the future in both regular and residential schools.	
	Career opportunities will likely expand as individuals with visual impairments become more aware of their legal and human rights.	

Guided Review

I. Definitions

   A. Legal Definition of Blindness

   - The legal definition is based on _____ and _____

   - A person whose visual acuity is 20/200 or less after the best possible correction with glasses or contact lenses is considered _____

   - A person whose vision is restricted to an area of _____ is considered legally blind.

   B. Educational Definitions of Visual Impairments

   - The IDEA definition emphasizes the relationship between _____

   - Totally blind: _____

   - Functionally blind: _____

   - Low vision: _____

   C. Age at Onset

   - Visual impairment can be _____ (present at birth) or _____ (acquired).

   - The age at onset has implications for how children with low vision should be taught.

II. Characteristics

   A. Cognition and Language

   - Impaired or absent vision makes it difficult to see the connections between experiences.

   B. Motor Development and Mobility

   - Visual impairment often leads to delays and deficits in motor development.

   C. Social Adjustment and Interaction

   - Children with visual impairments interact less and are often delayed in _____

   - Some individuals with visual impairments engage in _____ behavior.

   - Many persons who have lost their sight report that the biggest difficulty socially is dealing with _____

III. Prevalence

- Fewer than 2 children in 1,000 have visual impairments.

- Almost half of school-age children with visual impairments have at least _____

IV. Types and Causes of Visual Impairments

A. How We See

- Effective vision requires proper functioning of three anatomical systems: _____
  _____

- Six muscles attached to the outside of each eye enable it _____
  _____

- Inside the eye, tiny muscles adjust the shape of the lens in order to focus.

- The eye's nervous system converts light energy into electrical impulses and transmits that
  information to the brain, where it is processed into visual images.

B. Causes of Visual Impairments

- Refractive errors:_____

- Structural impairments: _____

- Cortical visual impairments: _____

V. Educational Approaches

A. Special Adaptations for Students Who Are Blind

- Braille is a tactile system of _____

- Braille technological aids have made braille more efficient, thus enabling many students to
  _____

- Declining braille literacy

- In response to the concern over declining braille literacy, the 1997 amendments to IDEA
  specified that IEP teams _____
  _____

- Tactile aids and manipulatives _____
  _____
  _____

- Technological aids for reading print include:_____

- Computer access

- Assistive technologies include: _____

B. Special Adaptations for Students with Low Vision

   1. Functional Vision

     - The fundamental premise underlying the development of functional vision is that

      _____

   2. Optical devices include: _____

   3. Reading Print

     - Students with low vision use three basic approaches for reading print:_____

      _____

     - In addition to print size, other equally important factors to consider are: _____

      _____

   4. Classroom adaptations include: _____

      _____

C. Expanded Curriculum Priorities

   1. Orientation and Mobility (O&M)

     - Orientation is _____

     - Mobility involves _____

     - O&M is considered a _____ by IDEA.

   2. Cane Skills

     - The long cane is the most widely used device for adults with severe visual impairments

      who _____

     - When properly used, the cane serves as both a _____

   3. Guide Dogs

     - Less than _____ of people with visual impairments travel with the aid of guide dogs.

   4. Sighted Guides

5. Electronic travel aids include: _____

6. Listening Skills

    *   A widely held misconception is that persons who are blind automatically _____

        _____

    *   The systematic development of listening skills is an important component of the

        _____

    *   Listening involves _____

        _____

7. Functional Life Skills

    *   Specific instruction and ongoing supports should be provided to ensure that students with

        visual impairments learn skills such as _____

        _____

VI. Educational Placement Alternatives

    *   Ninety percent of children with visual impairments are educated in public schools

    A. Itinerant Teacher Model

        *   Most students who are included in general education classrooms receive support from

            _____

        *   Some public schools have special resource rooms for students with visual impairments.

        *   The most important factor to the successful inclusion of students with visual impairments is

            the regular classroom teacher's _____

    B. Residential Schools

        *   About _____ of school-age children with visual impairments attend residential schools.

        *   The current population of residential schools consists largely of children with visual

            impairments with additional disabilities, such as _____

            _____

        *   Advantages of residential schools include _____

            _____

            _____

VII. Current Issues and Future Trends

    A. Specialization of Services

- Children with visual impairments are likely to receive special education services in the future in both regular and residential schools.

- Greater emphasis will be placed on intervention with infants and young children and on training older students for independence.

    B. Emerging Technology and Research

- It is hoped that all people with visual impairments will benefit from new technological and biomedical developments.

- Artificial sight may be possible in the future.

    C. Fighting against Discrimination and for Self-Determination

- Career opportunities will likely expand as individuals with visual impairments become more aware of their legal and human rights.

Homework

Write a 2- to 3-page position paper on one of the following topics.

1. Which child do you think would be more difficult to teach, the child with congenital blindness or the child with acquired blindness? Explain why.

2. It has been suggested that children with visual impairments are the easiest group of students with disabilities to integrate into the regular classroom. Would you agree or disagree with this statement? Explain.

3. Under what circumstances (if any) do you think a student with a visual impairment should attend a residential school?

4. Many people tend to underestimate the capacity of individuals with visual impairments. Consequently, people with visual impairments have been denied the full range of occupational and personal choices. What do you think the biggest hurdles are for people with visual impairments in obtaining and maintaining employment? Identify solutions to the problems of barriers to employment and meeting the specific needs of unemployed people with visual impairments.

Self-Check Quiz

True/False

1. Some students with visual impairments can learn to totally compensate for their vision loss by making use of their other senses.

2. In myopia, the eye is longer than normal, causing the image to fall in front of the retina.

3. Of visually impaired children in grades K through 12, three times as many read visually than read via braille.

4. Unlike other disabilities covered by IDEA, visual impairment has both legal and educational definitions.

5. By definition, a visual impairment requires that something be wrong with your eyes.

6. Stereotypical behaviors are seen in virtually all students with visual impairments at some point during their development.

7. Ninety percent of children with visual impairments are educated in public schools, with over half of them educated in regular classrooms at least part of the day.

8. As a general rule of thumb, when finding print reading materials for a visually impaired child capable of reading, the larger the print size, the better.

9. Zach is not considered legally blind because, with glasses, his visual acuity improves from 20/200 to 20/100.

10. Regarding classroom adaptations, the most effective low-vision device is proper light.

11. By default, a child who meets the federal definition of legally blind qualifies for special education.

12. Most children with visual impairments develop an increased sense of hearing to compensate for their loss of visual information.

13. Visual impairments in children preclude most incidental learning.

14. A child with low vision uses vision as a primary means of learning.

15. A person with 20/20 vision has perfect vision.

Essay Questions

1. Describe the basic premises they should have about low vision and its effects on a person as teachers develop curriculum and plan instruction.

2. Describe the expanded core curriculum for students with visual impairments, and give an example for each as might be provided to Tony, a 12-year-old student who became totally blind after a recent auto accident.

CHAPTER ELEVEN
PHYSICAL DISABILITIES, HEALTH IMPAIRMENTS, AND ADHD

Focus Questions

- **In what ways might the visibility of physical or health impairments affect a child's self-perception, social development, and level of independence across different environments?**

Earlier in the text the relative nature of disabilities was discussed—a disability might lead to educational, personal, or social problems in one setting, while in another setting the disability might not be handicapping at all. Although this is true for all disabilities, it may be more obvious for the child with a physical or health disability. For example, a child with an artificial limb may be handicapped when competing against nondisabled peers on the baseball field but may experience no handicap in the classroom. Also, students with physical disabilities will have different learning experiences in different environments depending upon how individuals in those environments act towards them. For example, students with physical disabilities are likely to have markedly different and perhaps more challenging outdoor experiences in a camp setting where counselors are comfortable working with them than in a camp setting where counselors are overly concerned about their physical or health disabilities. Likewise, a child with an invisible health impairment such as diabetes may encounter hostility from other students when he has to eat a snack during the middle of gym class if they do not understand the nature of this disability.

- **How do the nature and severity of a child's physical disability affect IEP goals and objectives?**

Students with physical disabilities may require modifications in the physical environment, teaching techniques, or other aspects of their educational programs. Some children with physical disabilities are extremely restricted in their activities, whereas others have few limitations on what they can do or learn. The goals and objectives of the IEP must match the individual needs of the child with physical disabilities. Modifications in the learning environment, including both physical and instructional adaptations, must be reflected in the IEP.

- **What are some of the problems that members of transdisciplinary teams for students with severe physical disabilities and multiple health needs must guard against?**

Members of transdisciplinary teams must guard against anything that interferes with open communication with one another. No other group of exceptional children comes into contact, both in and out of school, with as many different teachers, physicians, therapists, and other specialists. Because the medical, educational, therapeutic, vocational, and social needs of students with physical and health impairments are often complex and frequently affect each other, it is especially important that educational and health care personnel openly communicate and cooperate with one another.

- **How might an assistive technology device be a hindrance as well as a help?**

Special devices or adaptations often are necessary for children with physical or health impairments to function successfully. There is, however, an unfortunate side effect to them: their use makes the disability more conspicuous. The more conspicuous the disability, the more inclined others might be to react to the disability first and to the child as a person second. All children need to develop positive views of themselves, and inappropriate reactions from parents, teachers, classmates, and others have a decidedly negative impact on a child's self-esteem.

- **Of the many ways in which the classroom environment and instruction can be modified to support the inclusion of students with physical disabilities, health impairments, and ADHD, which are most important?**

Teachers of children with physical and health impairments frequently find it necessary to adapt equipment, schedules, or settings so that their students can participate more fully in educational and recreational activities. Although there is currently an increasing trend toward integrating children with physical and health problems, this practice has raised several controversial issues. These issues revolve around determining the extent to which teachers and schools should realistically be expected to care for students with physical and health-related disabilities. Decisions concerning the safety for all students must be made. Perhaps the most important classroom modification is creating an atmosphere in which the student with disabilities feels socially accepted and comfortable enough to learn and contribute.

Essential Concepts

- This chapter describes a population more different than alike. On one end of the spectrum are children with health problems but almost no physical limitations such as those with ADHD, asthma, hemophilia, or seizure disorders. On the other are children with physical impairments such as cerebral palsy, spina bifida, or muscular dystrophy. Many students with physical or health impairments do not have cognitive impairments and can learn at the same rate as their nondisabled peers, given the right accommodations and modifications. For no other group of exceptional learner is the continuum of educational services more relevant.

- The actual number of children with physical impairments and other health impairments is much higher than those receiving services in those categories. Many children are served under other categories. In addition, to qualify for special education services, the child's disability must adversely affect his or her educational performance.

- The three variables that are critically important in a child's development are the age at which the disability was acquired (prenatal, perinatal, or postnatal), the severity with which the condition affects different areas of functioning, and the visibility of the impairment.

- Educational approaches for these children often involve the collaboration of an interdisciplinary team of teachers; physical, occupational, and speech therapists; and other health care specialists. Children with physical disabilities may also need environmental modifications such as wheelchair-accessible classrooms or other assistive technology.

- How others react to a child with physical disabilities or health impairments is at least as important as the disability itself. In all cases it is important for teachers, classmates, and the general public to have an inclusive attitude toward this group of exceptional learners.

Objectives

PHYSICAL DISABILITIES AND HEALTH IMPAIRMENTS
1. List the key components of the federal definition of orthopedic impairment and other health impairments.
2. Discuss why there are more children with physical impairments and health care needs than those receiving services under those categories.
3. Compare and contrast a chronic condition and an acute condition that adversely affects educational performance.
4. Define and describe the types of physical disabilities discussed in this chapter.

ATTENTION-DEFICIT/HYPERACTIVITY DISORDER
1. List the defining characteristics of ADHD.
2. Describe the eligibility requirements for a student with ADHD to receive special educational services under existing categories or through Section 504 of the Rehabilitation Act.
3. List the possible causes of ADHD.
4. Describe the two main treatment approaches for ADHD.

CHARACTERISTICS
1. List the two characteristics that some children with physical disabilities and other health impairments share.
2. List the two factors that affect the impact of a physical disability or health impairment on a child's functioning.

EDUCATIONAL APPROACHES
1. Describe other professional's roles and responsibilities.
2. Discuss why collaboration and team work are especially important with this population of exceptional children.
3. Identify environmental modifications and assistive technology necessary to enable more full participation in school.

EDUCATIONAL PLACEMENT ALTERNATIVES
1. Identify and provide examples of the continuum of educational placement alternatives for children with physical impairments and special health care needs.

CURRENT ISSUES AND FUTURE TRENDS
1. Identify the key topics related to more full inclusion in society.
2. Describe the new and emerging technology for persons with severe physical disabilities.

Chapter Eleven at a Glance

Main Topics	Key Points	Key Terms
Physical Disabilities, Health Impairments, and ADHD	Children with physical disabilities and health impairments are eligible for special education under two disability categories: orthopedic impairments and other health impairments.	orthopedic impairment neuromotor impairment chronic conditions acute conditions
	Orthopedic impairments involve the skeletal system, and neuromotor impairments involve the nervous system.	
Physical Disabilities and Health Impairments	Physical disabilities and health impairments may be congenital or acquired, chronic or acute.	
	According to IDEA, a child is entitled to special education services if his or her educational performance is adversely affected by a physical disability or health-related condition.	
Prevalence	It is estimated that chronic medical conditions affect up to 20% of school-age children.	
Types and Causes	Cerebral palsy is a permanent condition resulting from a lesion to the brain or abnormality of brain growth.	cerebral palsy monoplegia hemiplegia triplegia quadriplegia paraplegia diplegia double hemiplegia spastic cerebral palsy athetoid cerebral palsy ataxic cerebral palsy hypotonia spina bifida occulta meningocele myelomeningocele hydrocephalus shunt generalized tonic clonic seizure absence seizure complex partial seizure simple partial seizure aura hypoglycemia hyperglycemia cystic fibrosis
	Spina bifida is a congenital condition in which the vertebrae do not enclose the spinal cord. Types of spina bifida include: spina bifida occulta, meningocele, and myelomeningocele.	
	Muscular dystrophy refers to a group of inherited diseases marked by progressive atrophy of the body's muscles.	
	Spinal cord injuries usually result in some form of paralysis below the site of the injury.	
	Epilepsy is characterized by various types of chronic and frequent seizures.	
	Diabetes is a chronic disorder of metabolism.	
	Asthma, cystic fibrosis, and HIV/AIDS may require special education and other related services.	
	Variables affecting the impact of physical disabilities on children's educational performance are severity, age at onset, and visibility.	

Chapter Eleven at a Glance

Main Topics	Key Points	Key Terms
Attention-Deficit/ Hyperactivity-Disorder	Persistent pattern of inattention and/or hyperactivity/impulsivity that is more frequent and severe than is typically observed in individuals at a comparable level of development.	
	It is estimated that 3% to 5% of all school-age children have ADHD.	
Characteristics	The characteristics of children with physical disabilities and health impairments are so varied that attempting to describe them is nearly impossible.	
	Factors that influence different areas of functioning include the severity of the disability, the age at onset, and visibility.	
Educational Approaches	Children with physical disabilities, health impairments, or traumatic brain injury require services from an interdisciplinary team of professionals.	transdisciplinary teams physical therapists occupational therapists orthotists prosthestists assistive technology
	Professionals who may be involved in providing services include: physical therapists, occupational therapists, speech-language pathologists, adaptive physical educators, school nurses, prosthetists, orthotists, health aides, counselors, and medical social workers.	
	Modifications to the physical environment and to classroom activities can enable students with physical and health impairments to participate more fully in the school program.	
	Assistive technology is any piece of equipment or device used to increase, maintain, or improve the functional capabilities of individuals with disabilities.	
	Students with physical limitations should be encouraged to develop as much independence as possible.	
Educational Placement Alternatives	About 40% of students with physical disabilities are served in regular classrooms.	medically fragile
	The amount of supportive help varies greatly according to each child's conditions, needs, and levels of functioning. Successful reentry of children who have missed extended periods of school requires preparation of the child, his or her parents, and school personnel.	
Current Issues and Future Trends	New and emerging technologies such as bionic body parts and robot assistants offer exciting possibilities for the future.	myoelectric limbs robotics
	Children with physical disabilities can gain self-knowledge and self-confidence by meeting capable adults with disabilities and joining self-advocacy groups.	

Guided Review

I. Physical Disabilities and Health Impairments

    A. Definitions

- Children with physical disabilities and health conditions who require special education are served under two IDEA disability categories: _____

- An orthopedic impairment involves the _____

- A neuromotor impairment involves the_____

- Children served under other health impairments have limited _____
_____

- Health impairments also include diseases that affect a child's _____

II. Prevalence

- It is estimated that chronic medical conditions affect up to _____ of school-age children

- Students with physical disabilities may be served under other categories, because their health impairments accompany other disabilities

- There are numerous children whose physical disabilities do not adversely affect _____
_____

III. Types and Causes

    A. Cerebral Palsy

- CP is the most prevalent physical disability in _____

- CP is a permanent condition resulting from _____
_____

- CP can be treated, but _____

- The term *plegia* is often used in combination with a prefix indicating the location of limb involvement (e.g., *paraplegia*, *quadriplegia*).

- Types of CP

    1. Spastic: _____

    2. Athetoid: _____

    3. Ataxia: _____

4. Rigidity and tremor: _____

- The Mobility Opportunities Via Education Curriculum is a _____
  _____

B. Spina Bifida

- Spina bifida is a condition in which the vertebrae do not enclose the spinal cord

- Spina bifida occulta: _____

- Meningocele:_____

- Myelomeningocele (most common, most serious):_____
  _____

- Hydrocephalus: _____

C. Muscular Dystrophy

- Muscular dystrophy refers to a group of_____

- At this time there is no known cure, and in most cases, this disease is fatal in_____
  _____

- Treatment focuses on maintaining function of _____

D. Spinal Cord Injuries

- _____ are the most common
  causes in school-age children

- The higher the injury on the spine and the more the injury cuts through the spinal cord, the
  greater _____

- Rehabilitation programs for children with spinal cord injuries usually involve _____
  _____

E. Epilepsy (seizures occur chronically and repeatedly)

- Generalized tonic-clonic seizure: _____

- Absence seizure: _____

- Complex partial: _____

F. Diabetes (chronic disorder of metabolism)

- Without proper medical management, the child's system is not able to obtain and retain adequate energy from food

- Hypoglycemia (low blood sugar) symptoms: _____

  _____

- Concentrated sugar ends the insulin reaction in a few minutes.

- Hyperglycemia (high blood sugar) symptoms: _____

  _____

- A doctor or nurse should be called immediately when a student shows symptoms of hyperglycemia.

G. Asthma: (chronic lung disease characterized by wheezing, coughing, and difficulty breathing)

- Most common _____ of children

- Leading cause of _____ in school

H. Cystic Fibrosis

- Genetic disorder in which the exocrine glands excrete thick mucus that can _____

- _____ are common characteristics of children with cystic fibrosis.

I. Human Immunodeficiency Virus and Acquired Immunodeficiency Syndrome

- Persons with AIDS are not able to fight off infections because of a breakdown of the _____

  _____

- HIV is transmitted through _____

- Children with HIV/AIDS legally cannot_____

- Because children with HIV/AIDS and their families often face discrimination, teachers and school personnel should actively facilitate _____

IV. Attention-Deficit/Hyperactivity Disorder

A. Definition and Diagnosis

- Persistent pattern of inattention and/or hyperactivity/impulsivity that is _____ than is typically observed in individuals at a comparable level of development

B. Academic Achievement and Comorbidity with Other Disabilities

- A large number of children with various disabilities are also identified as having ADHD.

C. Eligibility for Special Education

- ADHD is not a category recognized by IDEA, but it is estimated _____

  _____

- Children who are not served under IDEA are eligible for services under _____

  _____

D. Prevalence

- It is estimated that _____ of all school-age children have ADHD

E. Causes

- In most cases, the cause is _____

- Growing evidence that _____ may place individuals at a greater
  than normal risk of an ADHD diagnosis

- Neuroimaging technology shows that some individuals with ADHD have _____

  _____

F. Treatment

- Drug therapy and behavioral interventions

V. Characteristics

- The characteristics of children with physical disabilities and health impairments are_____

  _____

- Educational progress is hampered by_____

- Perform below average on social-behavioral skills

- Factors that influence different areas of functioning include _____

  _____

VI. Educational Approaches

A. Teaming and Related Services

- Physical therapists: _____

- Occupational therapists: _____

- Other specialists include _____

  _____

B. Environmental Modifications

- Environmental modifications include adaptations to provide _____

- Environmental modifications include assistive technology and special health care routines
  _____

VII. Educational Placement Alternatives

- About 40% of students with physical disabilities are served in _____

- The amount of supportive help varies greatly according to each child's _____
  _____

- Some technology-dependent children require _____
  _____

- Successful reentry of children who have missed extended periods of school requires preparation

  of _____

VIII. Current Issues and Future Trends

A. Related Services in the Classroom

B. New and Emerging Technologies for Persons with Severe Physical Disabilities

C. Animal Assistance

D. Employment, Life Skills, and Self-Advocacy

Homework

Write a 2- to 3-page position paper on one of the following topics.

1. Inclusion continues to be a major problem for students with physical disabilities. Children with physical and other health impairments are often placed in self-contained special education classes with children who have mental retardation. Do you think this is the best practice? What other options can school systems offer? How do you think general educators and parents feel about placing these children into the general education classroom? If you had a child with severe health impairment, what do you think would be the best placement?

2. Coping emotionally with a physical disability or health impairment presents a major problem for some children. Maintaining a sense of belonging can be difficult for a child who must frequently leave the classroom to participate in therapeutic or other health care routines. Differences in physical appearance and the need for assistive technology may further cause problems. What role and responsibility does the teacher play in creating an inclusive environment in the classroom? What do you think a teacher should do to help peers and others become more accepting of a student with a physical disability or health impairment?

3. The American Academy of Pediatrics (1994) recommends that most school-age children with HIV/AIDS be allowed to attend public schools without restrictions. Students with HIV/AIDS should attend the regular classroom and be provided with in-class supports (Prater & Serna, 1995). What kinds of school supports are most crucial for children with HIV/AIDS? If parents choose to inform the teacher that their child has HIV/AIDS, what are the roles and responsibilities of the teacher? Under what circumstances (if any) should children with HIV/AIDS be placed in environments that are more restrictive than the regular classroom?

Self-Check Quiz

True/False

1. Occupational therapists are involved in the development and maintenance of motor skills, movement, and posture.

2. Children with physical disabilities, health impairments, and traumatic brain injury are generally extremely restricted in their activities.

3. When Cheryl tries to sharpen her pencil, her arms wave wildly, she grimaces, and her tongue sticks out, probably indicating athetoid cerebral palsy.

4. A child with chronic asthma does well in school, but needs immediate assistance in the event he has a severe attack. By definition, he is eligible for services as health impaired.

5. Asthma is the leading cause of absenteeism in school.

6. A child with a neuromotor impairment receives service under IDEA as a child with an orthopedic impairment.

7. Children with contagious diseases, including HIV/AIDS and tuberculosis, were excluded from IDEA protection under the recent reauthorization.

8. Most traumatic brain injuries do not involve penetration of the skull.

9. The issue of inclusion of students with physical and health impairments is more one of technology than one of attitude.

10. Parents are required to inform the school if their child has HIV and certain other serious or contagious health conditions.

11. Related services are of particular importance to children with physical disabilities, health impairments, and traumatic brain injury.

12. Emily had a blow to the head and immediately suffered a seizure. By definition, she has epilepsy.

13. The term *medically fragile* refers to a student dependent upon life-support technology.

14. Recovery from a traumatic brain injury is consistent, i.e., slow at first and usually reaching a plateau, which signals the end to expected functional improvement.

15. School districts are not responsible for paying for services such as nursing care or catheterization because they are medical, not educational.

Essay Questions

1. Describe the characteristics, causes, effects, and treatments of either (a) epilepsy or (b) muscular dystrophy.

2. Describe Perrin et al.'s (1993) noncategorical system for classifying and understanding children's physical and medical conditions.

CHAPTER TWELVE
LOW INCIDENCE DISABILITIES: SEVERE/MULTIPLE DISABILITIES, DEAF-BLINDNESS, AND TRAUMATIC BRAIN INJURY

*Focus Questions*_____

- **Why is a curriculum based on typical developmental stages inappropriate for students with severe and multiple disabilities?**

Developmental theories of learning assume that children pass through an orderly sequence of developmental stages. These stages are the basis for determining what kinds of skills are appropriate for instruction and when those skills should be taught. For example, if a child has not yet developed the physical dexterity necessary to properly hold a pencil, teaching the child to write will usually not begin until the child is developmentally "ready." A curriculum based on typical developmental stages, however, is unlikely to meet the needs of students with severe disabilities. For children with severe disabilities, learning such basic skills as getting from place to place independently, communicating, controlling bowel and bladder functions, and self-feeding cannot wait for a readiness stage to be reached. Instruction in these skills, all of which influence the individual's quality of life, must begin when individuals with severe disabilities need to learn them, not when they are developmentally ready to learn them.

- **Why is it so critical to select functional and age-appropriate curriculum objectives for students with severe and multiple disabilities?**

Educational programs for students with severe disabilities are future oriented in their efforts to teach skills that will enable students to participate in integrated settings as meaningfully and independently as possible after they leave school. Functional and age-appropriate behaviors are more likely to be reinforced in the natural environments and, as a result, maintained in the student's repertoire.

- **Can a teacher increase the learning potential of students with severe and multiple disabilities? How?**

Absolutely! However, children with severe disabilities seldom acquire complex skills through imitation and observation alone. Therefore, instruction must be carefully planned, systematically executed, and continuously monitored for effectiveness.

- **What are the most important skills for a teacher of students with severe and multiple disabilities? Why?**

Teaching students with severe disabilities is difficult and demanding. The teacher must be well organized, firm, and consistent. He or she must be able to mange a complex educational operation, which usually involves supervising paraprofessional aides, student teachers, peer tutors, and volunteers. The teacher must be knowledgeable about instructional formats and be able to work cooperatively with other professionals. Teachers must also be sensitive to small changes in behavior.

- **How much time should students with severe and multiple disabilities spend in the general education classroom with their nondisabled peers?**

Although the social benefits of regular class participation for students with disabilities have been clearly shown, the effects of full inclusion on the attainment of IEP goals and objectives is not yet known. Available instruction time is especially valuable to students who, by definition, require direct, intensive, and ongoing instruction to acquire basic skills. A major challenge is to develop models and strategies for including students with severe disabilities without sacrificing opportunities to acquire, practice, and generalize the functional skills they need most.

Essential Concepts

- Often students with severe disabilities need instruction in many basic skills that most children acquire without instruction. However, it is well documented that these students can learn; do learn; and with appropriate teaching and support, lead productive lives.

- Today a philosophy of inclusion promotes the integration of individuals with severe disabilities into the mainstream of society. This trend is significantly different from the philosophy that promoted institutionalization from infancy.

- No universally accepted definition of severe disabilities exists, and this lack of a precise definition makes prevalence estimates difficult. Although no single set of behaviors is common to all individuals with severe disabilities, this population is often characterized by severe deficits in communication skills, physical and motor development, and self-help skills and by excesses of maladaptive or inappropriate behavior.

- The causes of severe disabilities are often traced to biological influences that result in brain damage. Chromosomal abnormalities, genetic disorders, complications during pregnancy or the birthing process, as well as head trauma and disease later in life can all cause severe disabilities. The specific cause of many severely disabling conditions, however, is not known.

- Educational programming for students with severe disabilities has changed dramatically from the not-so-distant past when automatic institutionalization and little or no instruction or training were the norm. Today, least restrictive educational placements are mandated, and the trend is toward educating students with severe disabilities in regular school settings.

- Individuals with severe disabilities present many challenges to the field of special education, but these challenges should not be viewed as burdens. Most of us do our best work when faced with challenges that demand our best. Educating students with severe disabilities is a dynamic, changing area of special education and one that influences the direction of the field as a whole. The opportunity to work with individuals with severe disabilities can provide tremendous personal and professional rewards.

Objectives

SEVERE AND MULITPLE DISABILITIES
1. Define *severe disability*.
2. Define *profound disability*.
3. Define *multiple disability*.
4. List the common characteristics of students with severe, profound, and multiple disabilities.

DEAF-BLINDNESS
1. Define *deaf-blindness*.

CHARACTERISTICS OF STUDENTS WITH SEVERE AND MULTIPLE DISABILITIES
1. List the seven most common characteristics of students with severe and multiple disabilities.

PREVALENCE OF SEVERE AND MULTIPLE DISABILITIES
1. List the justification for calling severe and multiple disabilities low incidence disabilities.

CAUSES OF SEVERE AND MULTIPLE DISABILITIES
1. List the probable causes of some types of severe disabilities.

TRAUMATIC BRAIN INJURY
1. List the key components of the federal definition of *traumatic brain injury.*
2. List the types and causes of brain injuries.
3. Describe the characteristics and educational needs of children with brain injury.

EDUCATIONAL APPROACHES
1. List the 3 questions that must be answered when considering curriculum.
2. List the major curriculum areas.
3. Identify and provide examples of effective instructional methods.
4. List the components of functional assessment.
5. Discuss the benefits to teaching students with severe disabilities in the local school.

THE CHALLENGE AND REWARDS OF TEACHING STUDENTS WITH SEVERE AND MULTIPLE DISABILITES
1. Discuss the challenges and reward of teaching students with severe and multiple disabilities.

Chapter Twelve at a Glance

Main Topics	Key Points	Key Terms
Low Incidence Disabilities		profound disabilities multiple disabilities deaf-blindness stereotypic behavior brain dygenesis
Severe and Multiple Disabilities	Severe disabilities are defined by significant disabilities in intellectual, physical, and/or social functioning.	
	Students with severe disabilities need instruction in basic skills, communicating with others, controlling bowel and bladder functions, and self-feeding.	
	Multiple disabilities means concomitant impairments, the combination of which causes such severe educational problems that they cannot be accommodated in a special education program solely for one impairment.	
Deaf-Blindness	The IDEA definition of deaf-blindness is a combination of both auditory and visual disabilities that causes severe communication and other developmental and learning needs.	
	The majority of children who have deaf-blindness at birth experience major difficulties in acquiring communication skills, motor and mobility skills, and appropriate social behavior.	
Characteristics of Students with Severe and Multiple Disabilities	Characteristics of severe disabilities include: slow acquisition rates for learning new skills, poor generalization and maintenance of newly learned skills, limited communication skills, impaired physical and motor development, deficits in self-help skills, infrequent constructive behavior and interaction, and stereotypic and challenging behavior.	
Prevalence of Severe and Multiple Disabilities	Because there is no universally accepted definition of severe disabilities, there are no accurate and uniform figures on prevalence. Estimates range from 0.1% to 1% of the population.	
Causes of Severe and Multiple Disabilities	In almost every case of severe disabilities, a brain disorder is involved.	
	A significant percentage of children with severe disabilities are born with chromosomal disorders or with genetic or metabolic disorders that can cause serious problems in physical or intellectual development.	
Traumatic Brain Injury	TBI is an acquired injury to the brain caused by an external physical force resulting in total or partial functional disability that adversely affects a child's educational performance.	open head injury closed head injury concussion contusions hemotoma coma
	Open head injuries are the result of penetration of the skull; closed head injuries are the result of the head hitting an object with such force that the brain slams against the inside of the cranium.	
	Impairments caused by brain injury may be temporary or lasting and fall into three main categories: physical and sensory changes; cognitive impairments; and social, behavior, and emotional problems.	

Chapter Twelve at a Glance

Main Topics	Key Points	Key Terms
Educational Approaches	Curriculum goals for students with severe disabilities should be functional and age-appropriate. Students with severe disabilities should be taught choice-making skills, communication skills, and recreation and leisure skills.	functionality partial participation positive behavioral support functional assessment
	Because each student with autism and severe disabilities has many learning needs, teachers must carefully prioritize and choose IEP objectives and learning activities that will be of most benefit to the student and his or her family.	
	Partial participation is both a philosophy for selecting activities and a method for adapting activities and supports to enable students with severe disabilities to actively participate in meaningful tasks that they are not able to perform independently.	
	The teacher of students with severe disabilities must be skilled in positive, instructionally relevant strategies for assessing and dealing with challenging and problem behaviors.	
	Elements of positive behavioral support include understanding the meaning that a behavior has for a student, teaching the student a positive alternative behavior, using environmental restructuring to make undesired behaviors less likely, and using strategies that are socially acceptable and intended for use in integrated settings.	
	Research and practice are providing increasing support for the used of integrated small-group instruction arrangements with students with severe disabilities.	
	Students with severe disabilities are more likely to develop social relationships with students without disabilities if they are included at least part of the time in the regular classroom.	
The Challenge and Rewards of Teaching Students with Severe and Multiple Disabilities	Although the initial reactions of many general education teachers are negative, those apprehensions often transform into positive experiences.	
	Teachers of students with severe disabilities must be sensitive to small changes in behavior.	
	The effective teacher is consistent and persistent in evaluating and changing instruction to improve learning and behavior.	
	Working with students who require instruction at its very best can be highly rewarding to teachers.	

Guided Review

I. Severe and Multiple Disabilities

- Most definitions are based on tests of _____

  _____

- Students with severe disabilities, regardless of age, need instruction in _____

  _____

- IDEA defines children with severe disabilities as those who need _____

- TASH definition: Individuals of all ages who require extensive ongoing support in more than one major life activity in order to participate in _____

II. Deaf-Blindness

- IDEA definition: _____

  _____

- The majority of children who have deaf-blindness at birth experience major difficulties in acquiring _____

III. Characteristics of Students with Severe and Multiple Disabilities

- Slow acquisition rates for _____

- Poor generalization and maintenance of _____

- Limited communication skills

- Impaired physical and _____

- Deficits in _____

- Infrequent constructive _____

- Stereotypic and _____

IV. Prevalence of Severe and Multiple Disabilities

- Because there is no _____ of severe disabilities, there are no accurate and uniform figures on prevalence.

- Estimates range from _____ of the population

V. Causes of Severe and Multiple Disabilities

- In almost every case of severe disabilities _____

- A significant percentage of children with severe disabilities are born with _____

  or with _____ that can cause serious problems in physical or
  intellectual development.

- Severe disabilities may develop later in life from _____

- In about _____ of all cases, the cause cannot be clearly determined

VI. Traumatic Brain Injury

A. Definition

- An acquired injury to the brain caused by an external physical force resulting _____

  _____

B. Prevalence of Traumatic Brain Injury

- It is estimated that each year, 1 in 500 school children will be hospitalized with traumatic
  head

  injuries, and 1 in 30 children will _____

- Leading cause of _____

- Most common acquired disability in childhood

C. Types and Causes of Traumatic Brain Injury

- Open head injury: _____

- Closed head injury: _____

- Concussion: _____

- Contusions: _____

- Hematoma: _____

- Severe head trauma almost always results in _____

D. Characteristics of Traumatic Brain Injury

- Impairments caused by brain injury may be temporary or lasting and fall into three main

  categories: _____

  _____

VII. Educational Approaches

    A. Curriculum: What Should Be Taught?

- Functionality

- Age-appropriateness

- Making choices

- Communication skills

- Recreation and leisure skills

- Prioritizing and selecting instructional targets

    B. Instructional Methods: How Should Students with Severe and Multiple Disabilities Be Taught?

- The student's current level of performance must be _____

- The skill to be taught must be _____

- The skill may need to be broken down into _____

- The teacher must provide _____

- The student must receive _____

- Strategies that promote _____

- The student's performance must be _____

    C. Where Should Students with Severe Disabilities Be Taught?

       1. Benefits of the Neighborhood School

- More likely to function _____

- Integrated schools are more _____

- Parents and families have _____

- Develop range of social relationships with _____

       2. Social Relationships

- Students with severe disabilities are more likely to develop social relationships with nondisabled students if _____

    _____

3. Experiences and Transformations of General Education Teachers

- Although the initial reactions of many general education teachers are negative, those apprehensions often transform into positive experiences

D. How Much Time in the Regular Classroom?

- A major challenge for both general and special educators is to develop models and strategies

for _____

VIII. The Challenge and Rewards of Teaching Students with Severe and Multiple Disabilities

- Teachers must be sensitive to _____

- The effective teacher is consistent and persistent in_____

_____

- Working with students who require instruction at its very best can be _____

_____

Homework

Write a 2- to 3-page position paper on one of the following topics.

1. Reread the Profiles & Perspectives feature, "Are All Children Educable?" Think about how your views about least restrictive environment, inclusion, and normalization have developed throughout the preceding chapters. How do your views about these issues change as the severity of an individual's disability increases?

2. Should skin shock be used to decrease or eliminate self-injurious behavior? Many children with severe disabilities engage in self-injurious behavior. The use of skin shock has been demonstrated to be effective for decreasing self-injury; however, the Association for Persons with Severe Handicaps (TASH) has been calling for the elimination of the use of all aversive procedures (including skin shock) to control individuals with disabilities. Explain the extent to which and under what circumstances (if any) self-injurious behavior should be controlled by skin shock or any other aversive procedure.

CD-ROM Questions

1. Give an original example of a service-learning project that could benefit students with disabilities and their community.

   School: Blendon Middle School
   Video and Commentaries: Service Learning

2. What does *reflective teaching* mean to you and what is its purpose?

   School: Blendon Middle School
   Video and Commentaries: Student Teacher & Student Teacher Feedback

3. What components and strategies are required to make inclusion of a student with severe disabilities a positive experience for all involved—the child with disabilities, his or her classmates without disabilities, teachers, parents, and family?

   School: Millennium Community School
   Video and Commentaries: All

Self-Check Quiz

True/False

1. The one defining characteristic of students with severe disabilities is that they exhibit significant and obvious deficits in multiple life-skill or developmental areas.

2. A brain disorder is involved in most cases of severe intellectual disabilities.

3. Children with profound disabilities are usually classified via intelligence tests.

4. Curriculum for students with severe disabilities should include functionality.

5. An open head injury is the most common type of head injury.

6. Recreation and leisure skills are a necessary part of a curriculum for children with severe disabilities.

7. IDEA specifies very limited circumstances under which a child is not considered educable (e.g., is comatose) and therefore not entitled to an education.

8. Students with severe disabilities should participate in activities that are appropriate for same-age peers without disabilities.

9. Geoff has blindness as well as cerebral palsy. He is best described as having severe disabilities.

10. There are crucial distinctions between children with profound disabilities and those with severe disabilities.

11. Research shows that full inclusion helps students with severe disabilities rapidly attain IEP goals and objectives.

12. Communication is independent of the specific mode that is used as a channel for communication.

13. The law requires that students with severe and multiple disabilities receive services in the least restrictive environment.

14. Relationship-based strategies are an important part of positive behavioral support.

15. Most severe disabilities are caused by trauma at birth or in later accidents.

Essay Questions

1. Discuss the relationship between a student's opportunity to make choices and his or her quality of life.

2. Describe the characteristics of individuals who are deaf-blind, and offer a rationale as to why this remains a separate disability category.

CHAPTER THIRTEEN
GIFTEDNESS AND TALENT

Focus Questions _____

- **Why do students who are very bright need special education?**

Special education is necessary for children when their physical attributes and/or learning abilities differ from the norm to such an extent that an individualized program of special education is required to meet their needs. When a traditional classroom curriculum is not allowing children who are gifted and talented to fulfill their potential and to succeed fully in school, then special education is needed.

- **How has the evolving definition of giftedness changed the ways in which students are identified and served?**

Intelligence, creativity, and talent have been central to the various definitions that have been proposed over the years, and they continue to be reflected in the current and still-evolving definitions. Historically, however, the concept of giftedness has been neither as broad nor as inclusive as the definitions we currently use. According to most early definitions, only those individuals with outstanding performances on standard intelligence tests were considered gifted. This narrow view of giftedness dominated by an IQ score prevailed for many years and came to be associated with only the Caucasian, urban, middle- and upper-class segments of society. Current definitions have grown out of our awareness that IQ alone does not define all the possible areas of giftedness. Today's definitions include many talents that contribute substantially to the quality of life for both the individual and society. This more comprehensive definition allows us to identify and serve a more diverse group of gifted learners.

- **What provisions should be made to accurately identify students with outstanding talents who are from diverse cultural groups or who have disabilities?**

Biases inherent in the identification process are primarily to blame for the underrepresentation of students from culturally diverse groups in programs for the gifted. Today more so than ever, we recognize the need for culturally nonbiased identification and assessment practices. Current best practices for identifying these students from diverse cultural groups involves obtaining information from a variety of sources such as portfolios of student work, tests in specific content areas, creativity tests, and problem-solving tests. Maker (1994) developed a procedure called DISCOVER that is used to assess gifted students from diverse backgrounds, female students, and students with disabilities. The DISCOVER assessment process involves a series of five progressively more complex problems that provide children with various ways to demonstrate problem-solving competence with the content and with one another.

- **How can the regular classroom teacher provide instruction at the pace and depth needed by gifted and talented students while meeting the needs of other students in the classroom?**

Three common approaches to educating students who are gifted and talented are curriculum compacting, enrichment, and acceleration. Each of these approaches can be used by the regular classroom teacher. Some experts advocate the development of an individualized growth plan to develop a broad program of services for gifted and talented students. The growth plan should include assessment information, student-generated goals, and the recommended activities for accomplishing these goals. A key ingredient of this approach is that the student is an active participant in all instructional and evaluative activities. Similar to the IEP, a growth plan could be used to guide the teacher in the development of appropriate lessons for the gifted and talented while at the same time meeting the needs of the other students. In addition, recent advancement in technology could be used to help further individualize the gifted student's program.

- **Should gifted students be educated with their same-age peers or with older students who share the same intellectual and academic talents?**

  Although ability grouping has been an issue of considerable debate, it is one strategy that might enable regular classroom teachers to appropriately differentiate instruction in order to meet the needs of the wide range of abilities represented in a classroom. Grouping enables gifted students to be appropriately challenged through more rapid and advanced instruction. Allowing gifted students to be grouped so that they can progress at their own pace may preserve the students' motivation to learn and help prevent problems such as boredom and an aversion towards school.

Essential Concepts _____

- Gifted and talented children represent the other end on the continuum of academic, artistic, social, and scientific abilities. Just as the traditional curriculum is often inappropriate for the child with a disability, it also can be inappropriate for the child who is gifted and talented. The traditional curriculum may not provide the kinds of challenges the gifted student requires to learn most effectively. As a result, these students may represent the most underserved group of exceptional children

- Numerous definitions of *gifted* and *talented* have been proposed and debated over the years. The first definitions focused solely on intellectual abilities as measured by IQ tests. More recent definitions have sought to encompass broader perspectives. The current definition has eliminated *giftedness* as a descriptive characteristic and further deemphasized IQ.

- Evidence of how the definition has changed is found in the way talented children are identified and assessed. Current assessment approaches are multifactored and include data from a variety of sources, including work portfolios, teacher and peer nominations, as well as traditional IQ and achievement tests. However, biases may still exist in the assessment process, as evidenced by the underrepresentation of some minority groups.

- Three common educational approaches for talented students are curriculum enrichment, compacting, and acceleration. Enrichment experiences are those that let students investigate topics of interest in much greater detail. Curriculum compacting is compressing the instructional content so that academically able students have more time to work on more challenging materials. Acceleration is the general term for modifying the pace at which the student moves through the curriculum.

- If the long-range needs of the society are to be met, it must capitalize on one of its most precious human resources—children who are gifted and talented. Given the opportunities to reach their potential, many of these children will contribute to the quality of our collective future. Of more immediate concern, and perhaps even more important, the educational needs of these exceptional children must be met because they are deserving of an appropriate education.

Objectives _____

DEFINITIONS
1. List the components of the federal (IDEA) definition of talented children.
2. Compare and contrast the Maker, Renzullli, Piirto, and Sternberg definitions of giftedness.

CHARACTERISTICS
1. Define and provide examples of common behavioral characteristics of students who demonstrate outstanding abilities.

PREVALENCE
1. List the prevalence figures for children who demonstrate outstanding abilities.

IDENTIFICATION AND ASSESSMENT
1. Identify the components of a multifactored assessment.

EDUCATIONAL APPROACHES
1. Define and provide examples of *curriculum enrichment*, *compacting*, and *acceleration*.

EDUCATIONAL PLACEMENT ALTERNATIVES AND ABILITY GROUPING
1. Describe the continuum of educational placements for students with EBD.

CURRENT ISSUES AND FUTURE TRENDS
1. Discuss the reasons that researchers deemphasize giftedness.

Chapter Thirteen at a Glance

Main Topics	Key Points	Key Terms
Giftedness and Talent Definitions	The federal definition of *gifted* and *talented* includes the following features: high performance capability in intellectual, creative, and/or artistic areas; an unusual leadership capacity; or excelling in specific academic fields. Other contemporary definitions of giftedness include Renzulli's three trait definition, Piirto's pyramid , and Sternberg's triachic model.	general intellectual ability specific academic talent
Characteristics	Children who are gifted rapidly acquire, retain, and use large amounts of information; relate ideas; make sound judgments; perceive the operation of larger systems; acquire and manipulate abstract symbol systems; and solve problems by creating novel solutions.	interindividual intraindividual divergent production fluency flexibility novelty/originality elaboration synthesizing ability analyzing ability
	The unusual talents and abilities of gifted students may make them either withdrawn or difficult to manage in the classroom.	
	Gifted and highly talented individuals are found across gender, cultural, linguistic, and disability groups.	
	Characteristics of highly gifted students (IQ > 145) may include intense intellectual curiosity, perfectionism, a need for precision, learning in intuitive leaps, intense need for mental stimulation, difficulty conforming, early moral/existential concern, and a tendency towards introversion.	
	Dimensions of creative behavior include fluency, flexibility, novelty/originality, elaboration, synthesizing ability, analyzing ability, ability to reorganized or redefine existing ideas, and complexity.	
Prevalence	The most commonly cited prevalence estimate is that high IQ students make up 3% to 5% of the population.	normal curve social construct
	There are many forms of talent that do not require a high IQ, 10% to 15% of students may possess such talents.	
Identification and Assessment	The usual method of identification in a multifactored assessment includes IQ tests; achievement tests; portfolios; and teacher, parent, self-, and peer nomination.	precocity
	Biases inherent in the identification process are primarily to blame for the underrepresentation of minority students receiving services for gifted education. Maker's DISCOVER procedure can be used to equitably identify students from diverse cultural groups.	

Chapter Thirteen at a Glance

Main Topics	Key Points	Key Terms
Educational Approaches	Curriculum for gifted students should be based on learning characteristics of academically talented students, possess academic rigor, be thematic and interdisciplinary, consider various curriculum orientations, and be balanced and articulated.	differentiated curriculum acceleration enrichment curriculum compacting tiered lessons Bloom's taxonomy interdependence
	Acceleration (moving through the curriculum faster) and enrichment (probing subject matter in greater depth) are ways to modify the curriculum for gifted students.	
	Curriculum compacting involves compressing the instructional content and materials so that academically advanced students have more time to work on challenging materials.	
	Tiered lessons provide different extensions of the same basic lesson for groups of students with differing abilities.	
	Bloom's taxonomy provides a framework for differentiating instruction and uses six levels of learning: knowledge, comprehension, application, analysis, synthesis, and evaluation.	
	Curriculum differentiation outside the classroom may include internships and mentor programs, special courses, competitions, summer programs, and international experiences.	
	Three models for differentiating curriculum include the Schoolwide Enrichment Model, Maker's active problem solver model, and the problem-based learning units.	
Educational Placement Alternatives and Ability Grouping	Students who are gifted may receive services in special schools, self-contained classrooms, resource rooms, and regular classrooms. There are advantages and disadvantages to each type of educational placement.	ability grouping tracking within-class grouping cluster grouping cross-grade grouping
	A teacher with special training may work with the regular classroom teacher as a consultant who collaborates to help plan multi-level lessons.	
	Many schools do not have a specialist, and the regular classroom teacher is responsible for differentiating the curriculum.	
Current Issues and Future Trends	The definitional nature of giftedness is being more intensely questioned.	
	We need better procedures for identifying, assessing, teaching, and encouraging these children. We must improve society's attitudes toward gifted and talented children if we are to improve their futures.	

*Guided Review*_____

I. Definitions

    A. Federal Definitions

- These children exhibit_____

  _____

- They require services or activities not_____

    B. Other Key Contemporary and Complementary Definitions

- Renzulli's three-trait definition: _____

  _____

- Piirto's pyramid model:_____

  _____

- Maker's problem-solving perspective

II. Characteristics

- Gifted and highly talented individuals are found across _____

  _____

- Characteristics of highly gifted students (IQ > 145): _____

  _____

    A. Individual Differences among Gifted and Talented Students

- Awareness of_____ is important in understanding gifted students.

    B. Creativity: dimensions of cognitive creative behavior

- Fluency

- Flexibility

- Novelty/originality

- Elaboration

- Synthesizing ability

- Analyzing ability

- Ability to reorganize or redefine existing ideas

- Complexity

III. Prevalence

- Gifted and talented children comprise about _____ of the school-age population.

- Gifted and talented children may be the most _____ of exceptional children.

IV. Identification and Assessment

- A multifactored assessment approach uses information from a variety of sources, including:

_____

_____

A. Multicultural Assessment and Identification

- Biases inherent in the identification process are primarily to blame for _____

_____

- Maker's DISCOVER procedure can be used to _____

_____

B. Gifted and Talented Girls

- Cultural barriers, testing and social biases, organizational reward systems, sex-role

stereotyping, and conflicts among career and family all _____

_____

C. Gifted and Talented Boys

- Problems include: _____

_____

D. Gifted and Talented Students with Disabilities

- The combination of a disability and giftedness brings with it an even more complicated _____

_____

V. Educational Approaches

A. Curricular Goals

Curriculum for gifted students should

- be based on learning characteristics of _____

- possess _____

- be thematic and _____

B. Differentiating the Curriculum: Acceleration and Enrichment

- Acceleration is the general term for _____

_____

- Enrichment means _____

_____

C. Lesson Differentiation in the Regular Classroom

- Curriculum compacting involves _____

_____

- Tiered lessons provide_____

_____

- Bloom's taxonomy provides a useful framework for differentiating instruction. The six levels
  of learning are: _____

D. Curriculum Differentiation Outside the Classroom

- Internships and mentor programs

- Special courses

- Junior Great Books

- Summer programs

- International experiences

E. Instructional Models and Methods

- The Schoolwide Enrichment Model

- Maker's active problem solver model

- Problem-based learning

VI. Educational Placement Alternatives and Ability Grouping

A. Special schools

B. Self-contained classrooms

C. Resource room or pull-out programs

D. Ability Grouping

- Most educators and researchers in the field of gifted education advocate for_____

- XYZ grouping or tracking places students into_____

- Potential dangers of tracking (low expectations, limited learning opportunities in lower tracks)

  have caused some critics to call for_____

- Students can also be grouped for instruction within a class or in cross-grade grouping for selected subjects (e.g., reading)

- Guidelines for ability grouping

  1. Resist calls for the wholesale_____

  2. Maintain programs of_____

  3. Maintain programs of_____

  4. Schools should try to adjust the curriculum to the_____

  5. Benefits are slight from programs that group children by ability but prescribe_____

      _____

VII. Current Issues and Future Trends

- The _____ nature of giftedness is being more intensely questioned.

- Most services for gifted and talented students will probably originate from the _____

- We need better procedures for identifying, assessing, teaching, and encouraging these children.

- We must improve society's attitudes toward gifted and talented children if we are to improve their futures.

Homework

1. Develop a brief assessment designed to measure creativity. After reviewing the definitions of each dimension of creativity identified by Guilford (1987) in Chapter 13, create one assessment task for each dimension. For example, *fluency* means the person is capable of producing many ideas per unit of time. So an example of an assessment for fluency might be, "Tell me as many uses for a paper clip that you can think of in one minute."

   - fluency
   - flexibility
   - novelty/originality
   - elaboration
   - synthesizing ability
   - analyzing ability
   - ability to reorganize or redefine existing ideas
   - complexity

2. As you read in this chapter, you *will* have gifted and talented students in your classroom. They are the most underserved population of special needs students. In order to meet their academic needs, you will have to differentiate. Choose a grade level, a subject, and a topic, and practice tiering a lesson. Include how you will assess the lesson. Alternately, you may choose to take a common story and practice your questioning techniques according to Bloom's taxonomy.

Self-Check Quiz

True/False

1. The universally accepted definition of *creativity* is that offered in Guilford's Structure of Intellect model.

2. Dion has the reading and writing abilities of a student 5 years older than himself but has mathematics abilities at grade level, reflecting intraindividual differences.

3. *Precocity* refers to achievements resembling those of older children.

4. The primary limitation of early federal attempts to define *giftedness* is that superior intellectual ability was the sole criterion.

5. Piirto's perspective is that the specific talents of highly gifted children should be nurtured toward careers productive for society, such as inventor, physician, artist, etc.

6. The current federal definition of *gifted and talented children* is not from IDEA, but rather the *National Excellence* report.

7. Giftedness ranks as the fourth largest group of children receiving special education services.

8. As criteria for identification of the gifted and talented have become less exclusive, it's likely that more children are identified than actually need services.

9. Each state has its own identification procedures and criteria for gifted and talented students.

10. Underrepresentation of children from groups such as African Americans and Latinos in gifted programs is primarily due to lack of parent and teacher initiation of the identification process.

11. An increasingly popular approach for identifying gifted and talented children is the multidimensional screening approach.

12. The incidence of giftedness and talent among a large proportion of students with disabilities is similar to that of the general population.

13. Curriculum compacting refers to a process of condensing material in scope and sequence.

14. Allowing a student to skip grades or to gain early entrance into college are examples of acceleration.

15. The concept of special schools for the gifted and talented has only recently been introduced, given that exceptionality historically emphasized disability.

Essay Questions

1. Compare and contrast the terms *acceleration* and *enrichment*, and provide two examples of each in practice.

2. Compare and contrast the Schoolwide Enrichment, Maker's active problem solver, and problem-based learning models of gifted education.

CHAPTER 14
EARLY CHILDHOOD SPECIAL EDUCATION

Focus Questions

- **Why is it difficult to measure the impact of early intervention?**

  Numerous methodological problems make it difficult to conduct early intervention research in a scientifically sound manner. Among the problems are selecting meaningful and reliable outcome measures; the wide disparity among children in the developmental effects of their disabilities; the tremendous variation across early intervention programs in curriculum focus, teaching strategies, length, and intensity; and the ethical concerns of withholding early intervention from some children so they may form a control group for comparison purposes.

- **How can we provide early intervention for a child whose disability is not yet present?**

  A child who has been identified as being at risk for developing a disability because of environmental or biological factors should receive preventive programming before any evidence of a disability exists. Parents and teachers do not have to wait until a delay in development occurs before they begin to interact with their children in ways that promote learning and development. Similarly, medical professionals do not need to wait and observe health or biological conditions before they can prescribe various precautionary or preventive procedures for the family to follow on behalf of the child. Intervention programs can never be started too early. Every reasonable precautionary and preventive measure that can be taken to ensure that the child does not develop a disability should be pursued.

- **Which do you think are the most important goals of early childhood special education?**

  The goals of early childhood special education are: (a) support families in achieving their own goals; (b) promote child engagement, independence, and mastery; (c) promote development in all important domains; (d) build and support social competence; (e) facilitate the generalized use of skills; (f) prepare and assist children for normalized life experiences with their families, in school, and in their communities; (g) help children and their families make smooth transitions; and (h) prevent or minimize the development of future problems or disabilities. After studying the goals, you should recognize that many are interrelated and all are intended to lead to increased independence and competency of individual children. All of the goals address the child within the context of the family and the community.

- **How does early childhood special education differ from special education for school-age children with disabilities?**

  Early childhood special education programs are administered by a state agency instead of the local school district. Young children qualify for early intervention services if there is severe developmental delay, a documented risk, or established medical conditions. Young children do not have to be identified under existing disability categories to be eligible for services. Additionally, a multidisciplinary team develops an individual family services plan that addresses the needs of the family as well as the child.

- **How can a play activity or everyday routine become a specially designed learning opportunity for a preschooler with disabilities?**

  Play provides children with natural, repeated opportunities for learning. Teachers of young children with disabilities can arrange the child's play environment to promote skill mastery across several developmental domains. Teachers must also monitor the child's progress and make adjustments to the environment that will facilitate success of important skills

Essential Concepts _____

- The first years of life are a critical period for children who are at risk for or have disabilities. Each month, the child risks falling further behind typically developing age mates if early intervention services are not provided. Early intervention services consist of educational, nutritional, child care, and family supports designed to reduce the effects of disabilities or prevent the development of problems later in life for children at risk. Repeated research clearly demonstrates that the sooner professionals and parents intervene with educational programs, the better the outcome for the exceptional child.

- IDEA guarantees a free, appropriate public education to all children. When it was originally passed, this law did not specifically require that preschool-aged children be served. Amendments to the legislation either mandated educational services or provided monetary incentives to provide those services.

- Involving the family in the assessment and treatment of infants and toddlers has become a crucial component of early childhood special education. In fact, IDEA mandates that the family is the recipient of educational services and an individualized family services plan (IFSP) must be developed for families of children receiving intervention services.

- Early intervention has begun to shift away from assessment instruments and procedures that are based entirely on developmental milestones and move towards curriculum-based assessment, which links testing, teaching, and new skill acquisition by the child. In other words, children are being assessed in terms of what they need to be able to do rather than how well their behavior corresponds to age-equivalent norms.

- Special education is known for its team approach to program planning. Nowhere is this more true or more important than in early childhood special education. The parents are encouraged to take an active role in their child's education, and they are often the recipients of services themselves. A child's progress might be quite difficult without parental assistance and insight. Both the support provided and needed by parents in early intervention programs is very important, and teachers must be sensitive to individual parents' limits of involvement.

Objectives _____

THE IMPORTANCE OF EARLY INTERVENTION
1. Define and describe early intervention services for children with or at risk for the development of disabilities.
2. Summarize the findings of early intervention research that has led to legislation mandating early intervention services.
3. List the outcomes for early intervention services identified by Congress.

IDEA AND EARLY CHILDHOOD SPECAL EDUCATION
1. List and describe the regulations pertaining to early childhood special education.
2. List and describe the four risk conditions that may entitle a young child to receive early intervention services
3. List the components of an IFSP.

SCREENING, IDENTIFICATION, AND ASSESSMENT
1. List and describe the four purposes of assessment and evaluation in early childhood education.
2. Identify examples of screening tools.
3. Identify examples of diagnostic tools.
4. Define and describe *curriculum-based measurement*.

CURRICULUM AND INSTRUCTION IN EARLY CHILDHOOD SPECIAL EDUCATION
1. List and describe the eight curriculum and program goals in early childhood special education.
2. Define and provide examples of *developmentally appropriate practice*.
3. Describe why curriculum based entirely on developmentally appropriate practice may not meet the needs of young children with disabilities.
4. List and describe the five quality indicators of IFSP goals and objectives.
5. Identify examples of curricular and instructional modifications.

SERVICE DELIVERY ALTERNATIVES FOR EARLY INTERVENTION
1. List and describe the types of service delivery options available in early childhood special education.

CURRENT ISSUES AND FUTURE TRENDS
1. List the two areas of need pertaining to research in early childhood special education.

Chapter Fourteen at a Glance

Main Topics	Key Points	Key Terms
Early Childhood Special Education	Early intervention consists of educational, nutritional, child care, and family supports designed to reduce the effects of disabilities or prevent the occurrence of developmental problems later in life for children at risk for such problems.	early intervention psychosocial disadvantage
The Importance of Early Intervention	Research has documented that early intervention can provide both intermediate and long-term benefits for young children with disabilities and those at risk for developmental delay. Benefits in early intervention include: gains in physical development, cognitive development, language and speech development, social competence, and self-help skills.	
IDEA and Early Childhood Special Education	P.L. 99–457 included a mandatory preschool component for children aged 3 to 5 with disabilities and a voluntary incentive grant program for early intervention services for infants and toddlers and their families. States that receive IDEA funds for early intervention must serve all infants and toddlers with developmental delays or established risk conditions. States may also serve infants and toddlers who fall under two types of documented risk: biological and environmental. The individual family services plan addresses the needs of the child and family. It is developed by a multidisciplinary team. Preschool children do not have to be identified under existing categories to receive services. Local education agencies may elect to use a variety of service options.	documented risk developmental delay established risk conditions biological risk conditions environmental risk conditions individualized family service plan (IFSP)
Screening, Identification, and Assessment	Assessment in early childhood special education is conducted for at least four different purposes: screening, diagnosis, program planning, and evaluation. Tests that seek to determine if a child is experiencing a developmental delay usually measure performance in 5 major developmental areas: motor development, cognitive development, communication and language development, social and emotional development, and adaptive development. Program planning uses curriculum-based, criterion-referenced assessments to determine a child's current skill level, identify IFSP/IEP objectives, and plan intervention activities. Many early intervention programs are moving away from assessments based entirely on developmental milestones.	screening diagnosis program planning Apgar scale

Chapter Fourteen at a Glance

Main Topics	Key Points	Key Terms
Curriculum and Instruction in Early Childhood Special Education	Curriculum and program goals for early intervention include: supporting families in achieving their own goals; promoting child engagement, independence, and mastery; promoting development in all important domains; building and supporting social competence; facilitating the generalized use of skills; preparing and assisting children for normalized life experiences with their families, in school, and in their communities; helping children and their families make smooth transitions; and preventing or minimizing the development of future problems or disabilities.	developmentally appropriate practice (DAP) embedded learning
	Developmentally appropriate practices provide a foundation on or context in which to build individualized programs of support and instruction for children with special needs.	
	IFSP goals and objectives should be evaluated according to the following five quality indicators: functionality, generality, instructional context, measurability, and relation between long-range goals and short-term objectives.	
	Modifications and adaptations to the physical environment, materials, and activities are often sufficient to support successful participation and learning by a child with disabilities.	
	Teachers should look and plan for ways to embed brief, systematic instructional interactions that focus on a child's IEP objectives in the context of naturally occurring activities.	
	Preschool activity schedules should include a balance of child-initiated and planned activities, large- and small-group activities, active and quiet times, and indoor and outdoor activities.	
Service Delivery Alternatives for Early Intervention	IDEA requires that early intervention services be provided in natural environments to the greatest extent possible.	hospital-based programs home-based programs center-based programs
	Service delivery options for early childhood special education include: hospital-based programs, home-based programs, center-based programs, and combined home-center programs.	
Current Issues and Future Trends	The field of early childhood special education will be advanced by research investigating which combinations of program characteristics are most effective for target groups of children and their families and from studies analyzing the cost-benefit of early intervention.	
	Parents are the most important people in an early intervention program. They can act as advocates, participate in educational planning, observe their children's behavior, help set realistic goals, work in the classroom, and teach their children at home.	

Guided Review

I. The Importance of Early Intervention

   A. Defining Early Intervention

- Early intervention consists of a wide variety of educational _____
  _____

- Home- and classroom-based efforts provide _____ services for at-risk children.

   B. Examining the Effectiveness of Early Intervention

     1. Research has documented that early intervention (Abecedarian Project, Project CARE, Infant Health and Development Program) can provide both intermediate and long-term benefits for young children with disabilities and those at risk for developmental delay.

     2. Congress identified the following outcomes for early intervention in the 1997 amendments to IDEA and the Individuals with Disabilities Education Improvement Act of 2004:

- To enhance the development of infants and toddlers with disabilities and to minimize their _____

- To reduce the educational costs to our society by _____

- To maximize the potential for _____

- To enhance the capacity of families_____

- To enhance the capacity of state and local agencies to _____
  _____

II. IDEA and Early Childhood Special Education

- P.L. 99–457 included a mandatory preschool component for children aged 3 to 5 with disabilities and a voluntary incentive grant program for infants and toddlers

   A. Early Intervention for Infants and Toddlers

- States that receive IDEA funds for early intervention must serve_____
  _____

- States may also serve infants and toddlers who fall under two types of documented risk:

  _____ *and* _____

     1. Developmental delays

2. Established risks conditions

3. Biological risk conditions

4. Environmental risk conditions

- The IFSP, a plan that addresses the needs of the child and family, is developed by a

  _____

- Unlike the IEP, an IFSP _____

  _____

  _____

- The IFSP must be evaluated once a year and reviewed at_____

B. Special Education for Preschoolers

- Preschoolers do not have to be identified and reported under existing disability categories to receive services

III. Screening, Identification, and Assessment

- Assessment in early childhood special education is conducted for at least four different purposes:

  _____

- Screening instruments include the _____

- Tests that seek to determine if a child is experiencing a developmental delay usually measure

  performance in 5 major developmental areas: _____

  _____

- A growing number of early intervention programs are moving away from assessments based

  entirely on developmental milestones to _____

IV. Curriculum and Instruction in Early Childhood Special Education

A. Curriculum and Program Goals

- Support families _____

- Promote child engagement _____

- Promote development in _____

- Build and support _____

- Facilitate the _____

- Prepare and assist children for _____

  _____

- Help children and their families make _____

- Prevent or minimize the development of_____

B. Developmentally Appropriate Practice

   Developmentally appropriate practice recommends the following guidelines for early childhood education programs:

   - Activities should be _____

   - Children's interests and progress should be _____

   - Teachers should arrange the environment to facilitate _____

   - Learning activities and materials should be _____

   - A wide range of interesting activities should be provided

   - The complexity and challenges of activities should _____

     _____

C. Selecting IFSP/IEP Goals and Objectives

   - Goals and objectives should be evaluated according to the following five quality indicators:

     _____

     _____

D. Instructional Adaptations and Modifications

   - _____to the physical environment, materials, and activities are often sufficient to support successful participation and learning by a child with disabilities

   - Embedded learning opportunities

E. Preschool Activity Schedules

   - Should include a balance of _____

     _____

F. A Supportive Physical Environment

- Designing an effective preschool program requires thoughtful planning to ensure _____

  _____

V. Service Delivery Alternatives for Early Intervention

- IDEA requires that early intervention services be provided in_____

  _____

- Service delivery options for early childhood special education include: _____

  _____

VI. Current Issues and Future Trends

- The field of early childhood special education will be advanced by research investigating the combinations of program characteristics that are most effective for target groups of children and their families and from studies analyzing the cost-benefit of early intervention

- _____ are the most important people in an early intervention program.

Homework

Write a 2- to 3-page paper on the following topic.

Almost all early childhood educators share a common philosophy that learning environments and teaching practices should be based on what is typically expected of and experienced by children at their developmental stages. This is called developmentally appropriate practice (DAP). Most early childhood special educators view the guidelines for DAP as providing a foundation on or context within which to provide early intervention services for children with special needs. However, a curriculum based entirely on DAP may not be sufficient for children with disabilities. Examine the list of guidelines for developmentally appropriate practice in Chapter 14, and write an explanation of the extent to which DAP guidelines can be modified or are appropriate for students with special needs.

CD-ROM Questions

1. How might a teacher use peers to enhance the effectiveness of a lesson in an inclusive classroom?

   School: Oakstone Academy
   Videos and Commentaries: Circle Time, Story Puppets, Peer Tutoring, & Fluency Building

2. What are the benefits for all children in an inclusive preschool classroom?

   School: Oakstone Academy
   Videos and Commentaries: Preschool Tour, Circle Time, Story Puppets, & Picture Schedules

3. How can a teacher tell if a child is ready to learn?

   School: Como Elementary
   Videos and Commentaries: All

Self-Check Quiz

True/False

1. Of all the people needed to make early intervention effective, parents are considered the most important.

2. Children must be classifiable by other IDEA disability categories (e.g., mental retardation, health impaired) in order to receive early intervention services.

3. Early intervention is sometimes provided to prevent the occurrence of learning and developmental problems in children at risk, even though a child may not currently exhibit deficits.

4. "Children learn by modeling" might be the best slogan for the National Lekotek Center.

5. Federal law currently requires that early intervention services be provided for infants and toddlers aged birth through 5 with disabilities.

6. Early intervention is often criticized for many reasons, including the possibility that the stigmatizing effect of labeling can lead to a self-fulfilling prophecy.

7. Transitions refer to a child and his or her family moving from one early intervention program or service delivery mode to another.

8. The term *developmentally appropriate practice* refers to procedural safeguards in assessment of young children.

9. There is little consensus among early childhood special educators on quality goals and objectives for young children in need of services.

10. Early childhood special education refers only to services that are classroom-based.

11. One outcome for early intervention is that it reduces educational costs to our society in the long run.

12. Severity of disability and intensity of intervention are the two factors most highly related to outcome effectiveness of early intervention.

13. Examples of skills in the adaptive domain include brushing teeth and dressing.

14. Curriculum-based assessment is an increasingly popular method for screening children.

15. The Milwaukee Project helps support maternal education and early infant stimulation as ways to reduce the incidence of mental retardation.

Essay Questions

1. What advice would you offer a parent in selecting toys for his or her young child with a disability?

2. Contrast IDEA requirements for service provision to children ages 3 to 5 with those for school-age children.

CHAPTER FIFTEEN
TRANSITIONING TO ADULTHOOD

Focus Questions _____

- **What can teachers of elementary children with disabilities do to help prepare them for successful lives as adults?**

  According to IDEA, a statement of transition service needs must be included in the student's IEP beginning at age 14, and an individualized transition plan must be developed by age 16. However, preparing students with disabilities to function successfully in the real world should begin as early as possible. Teachers can begin preparing elementary children with disabilities for adulthood by targeting skills such as social interaction, functional academics (e.g., telling time, counting money), daily living (e.g., eating habits, self-care), and choice making. Additionally, teachers should expose students to the variety of career opportunities and leisure activities available to them.

- **Why should postschool outcomes drive education programming for secondary students with disabilities?**

  When developing an individualized transition plan for secondary students with disabilities, the question guiding the selection of each objective should be, "Will the student need this skill when he or she is 21?" The goal of transition planning is to enable students to function as independently as possible when they become adults. The multidisciplinary team should select only the goals and objectives that will contribute to the postschool success of students with disabilities.

- **What are the most important factors in determining the success of an individualized transition plan?**

  Nowhere in special education are teaming and collaboration more important than they are when planning and delivering services for secondary students. The factors most likely to determine the success of an individualized transition plan include the student's involvement, family involvement, and collaboration by the professionals involved. Cooperation and communication between and among professionals and families are critical to effective transition planning.

- **How can programs that are intended to help adults with disabilities limit their participation and enjoyment of adulthood?**

  In the process of creating teaching and working environments that promote success for individuals with disabilities, we sometimes fail to adequately prepare them to live and work in more normalized settings. How? We create teaching and learning environments that are significantly different than more normalized settings. As a result, attempts at integration into normalized settings are often unsuccessful. Even though all individuals with disabilities will not likely achieve full independence in their communities, special education must plan its instruction to provide every opportunity for the achievement of independent adult living by individuals with disabilities.

- **Should quality of life for adults with disabilities be the ultimate outcome measure for special education?**

  Ultimately, quality of life should be the outcome measure of all educational programs, including those programs for students with disabilities. A person may have been taught many skills, but if those skills do not enable him or her to enjoy the benefits available in personal, social, work, and leisure settings, the wrong skills have been taught and a disservice has been done to that individual. When selecting and prioritizing specific skills to teach students with disabilities, teachers must consider the extent to which those skills will ultimately help improve the student's quality of life.

Essential Concepts _____

- Although American society has come a long way in regard to the opportunities afforded young adults with disabilities, it has been estimated that as many as 30% of special education students drop out of school before graduation. In addition, former special education students are more likely to be under- or unemployed after they exit school than are non–special education age mates. Thus, there is a long way to go in developing effective transition-to-adulthood programming and in improving society's attitudes toward the integration of adults with disabilities into work settings.

- Because so many professionals have dedicated themselves to learning more about effective programming for transition into adulthood, there are more exceptional adults than ever working, living, and enjoying leisure activities in community-based, integrated settings. In the not-too-distant past, the opportunity for adults with disabilities to earn competitive wages for meaningful work was almost nonexistent. Today, a type of vocational opportunity referred to as supported employment enables individuals with severe disabilities to participate successfully in integrated settings.

- In addition to educating individuals with disabilities in work and independent-living skills, many professionals realize the importance of teaching recreation and leisure skills. Learning appropriate recreational and leisure-time activities is difficult for many adults with disabilities.

- Increased community-based residential services for adults with disabilities have meant a greater opportunity to live in more normalized settings. Three residential alternatives for adults with mental retardation and related developmental disabilities—group homes, foster homes, and semi-independent apartment living—help to complete the continuum of possible living arrangements between the segregated public institution and fully independent living.

- The quality of life for most adults with disabilities in the new millennium is better than it has ever been. Over the past 25 years, adults with mental retardation have been moving from large institutions into smaller, more normalized, community-based living environments. Increasingly, these adults are employed in integrated settings. Special education has come a long way in educating exceptional children to be better prepared for the challenges and joys of being an adult. In addition, society at large is providing more of the same opportunities to these adults. However, there remains much work to be done.

Objectives _____

HOW DO FORMER SPECIAL EDUCATION STUDENTS FARE AS ADULTS?
1. List the outcome data from the National Longitudinal Transition Study (NLTS) on how former special education students fare as adults.

TRANSITION SERVICES AND MODELS
1. Describe Will's Bridges model of school-to-work transition.
2. Describe Halpern's three-dimensional model of transition.
3. List the components of an individualized transition plan.
4. Discuss the importance of collaboration and teaming.
5. Define and describe *transition planning* and when it should begin.

EMPLOYMENT
1. Describe the range of employment options for special education students.
2. Discuss the benefits and drawbacks of each employment option.

POSTSECONDARY EDUCATION
1. List the data for the number of special needs students attending postsecondary school.

RESIDENTIAL ALTERNATIVES
1. Describe the range of living arrangement alternatives available to adults with disabilities.

RECREATION AND LEISURE
1. Discuss the importance of teaching recreation and leisure skills.

THE ULTIMATE GOAL: A BETTER LIFE
1. List the areas that need improvement if students with special needs are to become more productive members of society.

Chapter Fifteen at a Glance

Main Topics	Key Points	Key Terms
Transitioning to Adulthood		
How Do Former Special Education Students Fare as Adults?	The unemployment rate for young adults with disabilities who have been out of school for less than two years is 46%, and it is 36.5% when they have been out of school for 3 to 5 years.	
	Most young adults who had found competitive employment were working part-time, low-paying jobs.	
	The percentage of college students who indicate they have a disability has increased in recent years. Compared to their peers without disabilities, however, fewer former special education students pursue postsecondary education.	
	Four out of five former special education students had still not achieved the status of independent adulthood after being out of high school for up to 5 years.	
Transition Services and Models	Transition from school to life in the community has become perhaps the most challenging issue in special education today.	individualized transition plan
	Models for school-to-adult-life transition stress the importance of a functional secondary school curriculum that provides work experience in integrated community job sites, systematic cooperation between school and adult service agencies, parental involvement and support, and a written individualized transition plan to guide the entire process.	
	Examples of transition models are Will's Bridges model of school-to-work transition and Halpern's three-dimensional model.	
	Transition services, as defined in IDEA, are an outcome-oriented process based upon individual needs; they include instruction, related services, community experiences, employment, and daily living and functional vocational evaluation.	
	When a student reaches age 14, IDEA requires the IEP team to consider postschool goals; and at age 16, an individualized transition plan must be developed.	
Employment	A person who is competitively employed performs work valued by an employer, functions in an integrated setting with nondisabled co-workers, and earns at or above the minimum wage.	competitive employment supported employment mobile work crew enclave natural supports self-management sheltered workshop
	Supported employment is competitive work in integrated settings for persons with severe disabilities, for whom competitive employment has not traditionally occurred, and who need intensive support services or extended services in order to perform such work.	

Chapter Fifteen at a Glance

Main Topics	Key Points	Key Terms
Employment (continued)	Four models of supported employment include small business enterprise, mobile work crew, enclave or workstation, and individual placement.	work activity center contracting prime manufacturing reclamation
	Sheltered employment is a vocational setting for adults with disabilities that offers transitional and extended employment. The problems with sheltered employment include limited opportunities for job placement and low pay.	
Postsecondary Education	Postsecondary education significantly improves the chances of meaningful employment.	
	Increasingly, jobs require technical training, problem-solving, and interpersonal skills that can be attained through postsecondary education.	
Residential Alternatives	Historically, segregation and institutionalization were the only options for persons with severe disabilities.	group homes foster homes apartment cluster co-residence apartment maximum independence apartment supported living deinstitutionalization
	Today most communities provide a variety of residential options, including groups homes, foster homes, and various types of apartment living.	
	Supported living is the term used to describe a growing movement of helping people with disabilities live in the community as independently and normally as they possibly can.	
	Supported living is guided by individualization; future planning; use of connections; flexible supports; combining natural supports, learning, and technology; focusing on what people can do; using language that is natural to the setting; and ownership and control.	
	Deinstituationalization, the movement of people with mental retardation out of large institutions and into small community-based living environments, has been an active reality for the past 30 years.	
Recreation and Leisure	Learning to participate in age-appropriate recreation and leisure activities is necessary for a self-satisfying life style.	
The Ultimate Goal: A Better Life	Adults with disabilities continue to face lack of acceptance as full members of society.	handicapism self-advocacy
	Handicapism, the discriminatory treatment and biased reactions toward someone with a disability, occurs on personal, professional, and societal levels.	
	Persons with disabilities have begun to assert their legal rights and challenge the view that persons with disabilities are incapable of speaking for themselves.	

Guided Review

I.   How Do Former Special Education Students Fare As Adults?

   A. Completing High School

      • Special education students who do not complete high school are more likely to have lower

         levels of _____ and higher rates of _____

   B. Employment

      • Data from NLTS show an unemployment rate of 46% for all youth with disabilities who have
        been out of school less than 2 years; this rate then drops to _____ when they have been out
        of school 3 to 5 years

   C. Postsecondary Education

      • Twenty-seven percent of young adults with disabilities are enrolled in postsecondary
        education programs within 3 to 5 years after leaving school, compared with _____ of
        the general population.

   D. Overall Adjustment and Success

      • After being out of high school for 3 to 5 years, only 37% of youth with disabilities were living
        independently, compared with _____ of the general population.

II. Transition Services and Models

   A. Will's Bridges Model of School-to-Work Transition

   B. Halpern's Three-Dimensional Model

   C. Definition of Transition Services in IDEA

      • Outcome-oriented process; based upon individual needs; includes _____

         _____

   D. Individualized Transition Plan

      • When a student reaches age 14, IDEA requires the IEP team to_____

      • When a student reaches age 16, a(n)_____

   E. Transition Teaming

      • Transition involves the _____

         _____

F. Beginning Transition Activitiew and Career Education Early

- Appropriate transition-related objectives should be selected at each age level, beginning in_____

III. Employment

  A. Competitive Employment

- A person who is competitively employed performs work valued by an employer _____

     _____

     _____

- Three characteristics of good secondary programs: _____

     _____

  B. Supported Employment

- Supported employment is competitive work in integrated settings for persons with severe disabilities, for whom competitive employment has not traditionally occurred and for whom

     _____

- Types of supported employment include: _____

     _____

  C. Sheltered Employment

- _____ in segregated settings are the most common types of vocational activities for adults with severe disabilities.

- Sheltered workshops provide three types of programs:_____

     _____

- The problems with sheltered employment include:_____

     _____

IV. Postsecondary Education

- Postsecondary education significantly improves the chances of _____

- Even youth with moderate and severe disabilities can _____

V. Residential Alternatives

- Historically, segregation and _____ were the only options for persons with severe disabilities.

- Today most communities provide a variety of _____ for people with disabilities

A. Group Homes

    - Group homes provide _____

    - During the day, most residents _____

B. Foster Homes

    - As part of a family unit, the adult with disabilities also _____

    _____

C. Apartment Living

    - Apartment living offers a greater opportunity for integration into the community than group homes

    - Three types of apartment living for adults with disabilities are: _____

    _____

D. Supported Living

    - *Supported living* is the term used to describe _____

    _____

    - Supported living is guided by the following principles: individualization; future planning; ___

    _____

    _____

E. Institutions

    - The inherent inability of institutional environment to_____

    _____

    - Deinstituationalization is_____

    _____

VI. Recreation and Leisure

    - Recreation and leisure activities do not come easily for many adults with disabilities.

    - Too often, leisure time of adults with disabilities is spent _____

    - Special educators must realize the importance of including training for recreation and leisure for school-age children with disabilities

VII. The Ultimate Goal: A Better Life

    A.   Quality of Life: _____

       _____

    B.   Misguided and Limiting Presumptions:_____

       _____

    C.   Self-Advocacy and Self-Determination: _____

       _____

    D.   Still a Long Way to Go

Homework

Write a 2-page position paper on one of the following topics.

1. Identify the most critical barriers to employment for adults with disabilities. Suggest strategies for overcoming the barriers to employment at the societal level and at the individual level.

2. Discuss the issues surrounding the right to get married and raise children for people with disabilities.

3. What are the most important indicators of quality of life for adults with disabilities? According to your text, "Most advocates and professionals now realize that the physical presence of individuals with disabilities in integrated residential, work, and community settings is an important first step but that the only truly meaningful outcome of human service programs must be an improved quality of life." Explain your conception and definition of "quality of life." Explain how quality of life can be measured within the context of your definition, and make recommendations about what must be done to improve the quality of life for adults with disabilities.

Self-Check Quiz

True/False

1. Sheltered workshops are considered an appropriate transition outcome for most students with disabilities.

2. An increasing self-advocacy is demonstrating that many persons with disabilities have the self-determination to speak for themselves.

3. The primary focus of transition planning is on establishment of postsecondary supports to foster success.

4. It is better to teach leisure and recreation skills that are commensurate to a person's mental age rather than their chronological age.

5. Career education for the disabled is a process begun at birth and continuing throughout life.

6. IDEA requires that transition planning begin when a student reaches the age of 14.

7. Co-worker involvement is important in supported employment, because co-workers can fix any errors the person with a disability may have made.

8. The primary characteristics of group homes that make them effective are their small size and residential location.

9. Institutions are generally considered an outdated and inappropriate residential option for individuals with disabilities.

10. Only about 30% of students with disabilities complete high school; within 5 years, however, about 25% complete a program to earn a diploma or GED.

11. Co-workers leaving their station to go on break is an example of a natural cue.

12. Reese is competitively employed by ProData, a company that pays him and other deaf students to write computer code for $20 an hour in an unsupervised setting.

13. IDEA requires transitional services for youth with disabilities.

14. The two primary criteria for having a high quality of life are living in a community-based residence and working in an integrated setting.

15. The percentage of college students who indicate they have a disability has increased in recent years.

Essay Questions

1. Compare and contrast models of supported employment, then highlight the ways in which they differ from competitive employment.

2. For an individual with disabilities working in a grocery store, provide (a) three examples of natural cues, (b) an example of self-monitoring, and (c) an example of self-evaluation that they might use.

Answers to Self-Check Quizzes

Chapter 1
1. F; 2. F; 3. F; 4. T; 5. F; 6. T; 7. T; 8. F; 9. F; 10. T; 11. F; 12. T; 13. F; 14. T; 15. T

Chapter 2
1. F; 2. F; 3. T; 4. F; 5. T; 6. T; 7. T; 8. F; 9. T; 10. F; 11. T; 12. T; 13. F; 14. F; 15. T

Chapter 3
1. F; 2. F; 3. T; 4. F; 5. T; 6. F; 7. T; 8. T; 9. T; 10. F; 11. T; 12. F; 13. F; 14. F; 15. F

Chapter 4
1. T; 2. T; 3. T; 4. F; 5. T; 6. F; 7. F; 8. T; 9. F; 10. T; 11. T; 12. T; 13. F; 14. F; 15. T

Chapter 5
1. T; 2. F; 3. T; 4. F; 5. F; 6. F; 7. T; 8. F; 9. F; 10. F; 11. T; 12. F; 13. T; 14. F; 15. T

Chapter 6
1. T; 2. T; 3. F; 4. F; 5. F; 6. T; 7. T; 8. F; 9. T; 10. T; 11. F; 12. F; 13. F; 14. F; 15. T

Chapter 7
1. T; 2. T; 3. F; 4. T; 5. T; 6. F; 7. F; 8. T; 9. F; 10. F; 11. F; 12. T; 13. F; 14. T; 15. F

Chapter 8
1. F; 2. T; 3. T; 4. F; 5. T; 6. T; 7. F; 8. T; 9. F; 10. F; 11. F; 12. T; 13. F; 14. F; 15. T

Chapter 9
1. T; 2. T; 3. T; 4. T; 5. F; 6. T; 7. F; 8. F; 9. T; 10. F; 11. T; 12. T; 13. T; 14. F; 15. T

Chapter 10
1. T; 2. F; 3. F; 4. T; 5. F; 6. F; 7. T; 8. T; 9. F; 10. T; 11. F; 12. T; 13. F; 14. F; 15. T

Chapter 11
1. F; 2. T; 3. T; 4. T; 5. F; 6. F; 7. T; 8. F; 9. T; 10. T; 11. F; 12. F; 13. T; 14. T; 15. F

Chapter 12
1. F; 2. F; 3. T; 4. F; 5. T; 6. T; 7. F; 8. T; 9. F; 10. F; 11. T; 12. F; 13. T; 14. F; 15. F

Chapter 13
1. F; 2. F; 3. F; 4. T; 5. F; 6. T; 7. F; 8. T; 9. F; 10. T; 11. F; 12. T; 13. F; 14. F; 15. F

Chapter 14
1. F; 2. T; 3. T; 4. F; 5. F; 6. T; 7. F; 8. F; 9. T; 10. F; 11. T; 12. T; 13. F; 14. T; 15. F

Chapter 15
1. F; 2. T; 3. F; 4. F; 5. T; 6. T; 7. F; 8. T; 9. F; 10. F; 11. T; 12. F; 13. T; 14. F; 15. T